· CROCHET ·
ILLUSION
— BLANKETS —

15 patterns for optical illusion crochet
blankets, afghans and throws

HELEN SMITH

DAVID & CHARLES

www.davidandcharles.com

CONTENTS

INTRODUCTION

Hello and welcome to my book, *Crochet Illusion Blankets*. My name is Helen and I have passion for anything crochet related! I am a mum of two beautiful daughters and a wife to my lovely husband. My husband is the reason why I first picked up a crochet hook: we were holidaying in North Wales for his 40th birthday and we went into a lovely little shop that had lots of wool and hooks and I decided to give it a go because I have always admired the art of crochet, just never tried it. I then watched a YouTube video back at our holiday house and made a hat for each of my daughters, and I have never looked back. It's pretty unusual for me if I don't do some sort of crochet each day with my two little doggies by my side.

I have a varied background in crochet, but my first love is blankets and I just love that I can make an idea in my head into a reality, and sometimes even make a drawing come to life through crochet. I started designing back in 2020 when we were all going through lockdown. Since then my work has been in several crochet magazines, I've been a guest designer for Bella Coco Crochet, I've designed blankets and other items for yarn brands, and the contents for a monthly subscription box for the Crochet Society. However, my biggest achievement to date is in writing this book, and I have to pinch myself every time I remember that I am on this amazing journey. I will be forever grateful for everyone's help and support.

But where did the idea of illusion crochet come from? Well, it all started with the memory of something I used to study in maths at school, called parabolic curves. I used to draw them all the time at home in so many variations, and when I took up designing crochet, I decided to try and recreate a parabolic curve in the form of a blanket design. That's when my crochet illusion blanket idea was born!

This book contains everything you need to know about making the 15 crochet illusion blanket projects. Each blanket is created using the intarsia crochet technique and through the course of the book I will not only explain this technique, but also take a look at how to choose colours that will work and explain how to arrange your yarn while making a blanket. Each pattern includes full written instructions as well as a colour chart. The best thing about the blankets, though, is that all of them are made with the same stitch, and it's simply the clever arrangement of the changing colours that creates the beautiful optical illusions!

TOOLS AND MATERIALS

Here, you'll find a list of the tools and materials you will need to make your own illusion blankets. Each blanket in the book is made with the same yarn brand and weight (aran/worsted) throughout, but you could use any brand or weight, just as long as you take the time to calculate the amount of yarn you will need to make your blanket. If you decide to use a lighter weight yarn, for example DK (light worsted), then your blanket will be smaller in size, but you may not need the same yarn quantities as advised for each blanket.

YARN

For all the projects in this book I've used Scheepjes Truly Scrumptious (50% recycled polyester (from recycled plastic bottles) and 50% acrylic), aran (worsted) weight, 100g (3½oz) = 108m (118yd), in the following shades:

A: Buttercream Icing (302)

B: Cotton Candy Meringue (330)

C: Rose Barfi (321)

D: Orange Cheesecake (332)

E: Custard Pie (341)

F: Pistachio Bundt Cake (318)

G: Mint Whoopie Pie (340)

H: Bubblegum Ice Cream (355)

I: French Blue Macaron (343)

J: Lavender Slice (334)

K: Sweet Potato Mochi (320)

HOOKS

Crochet hooks are available in several different materials, from bamboo and plastic to aluminium and even casein, which is a milk protein. Which material you choose is down to personal preference, but also texture – for example, bamboo hooks may be slightly less smooth than metal or plastic, so it's best not to pair them with a rougher or hairier yarn as there'll be too much friction.

All of the blankets in this book were made with a 6.5mm (US K/10.5) Clover Amour crochet hook. This is very comfortable hook, with a lovely ergonomic design and a colourful rubber handle that sits very nicely in the hand while crocheting. It is also very lightweight, which helps when changing colours. I would definitely recommend trying out some different hooks to find a nice, comfortable hook to make your blankets with.

OTHER EQUIPMENT

You'll also need the following items in order to complete the blankets:

- Scissors
- Tapestry/yarn needle
- 7cm (2¾in) pompom maker (optional)

All of these items will be readily available in your local crafts store or haberdashery.

INTARSIA CROCHET

I'm sure you're keen to get started, but before you grab your hook, read through this section on intarsia crochet, which will explain how to work the technique, how to join in different yarn colours and, most importantly, how to manage your yarn as you work. Intarsia crochet requires lots of small yarn balls to be attached to your blankets as you work on them, so it's essential to manage them effectively to avoid a tangle.

Have you tried intarsia crochet before? If not, don't worry, it will all be explained! If you have tried tapestry crochet you may find intarsia similar, with the main difference being that instead of the yarn being carried through the work, it is dropped at the back of the blanket to be picked up again when needed. It may seem fiddly at first, but the fact that only one simple stitch is used throughout each pattern means these projects are beginner friendly.

If you haven't tried any crochet colourwork before, then the blankets in this book are a good place to start, and you will easily pick up the intarsia crochet technique as you work. The only stitch you need to be familiar with is the HDC—Half Double Crochet stitch (US term). You will also need to be familiar with the right side and wrong side of your blanket – see Right Side or Wrong Side? for more information.

HOW IT WORKS

The creative possibilities of intarsia crochet are endless because it can be worked with as few as two colours, up to however many you like. Intarsia involves using multiple lengths of individual, different coloured yarns to create distinct patterns, such as the mesmerizing, op-art-inspired designs in this book.

Yarn colours are dropped (fastened off) and picked up (reattached) as you need them in the pattern. This means that intarsia crochet is the perfect technique for the illusion blankets.

CHOOSING COLOURS

If it's new to you, working with colour and choosing colours can sometimes be scary. I LOVE working with colour and find I get inspiration from all kinds of things in my everyday life, from a lovely sunset to a bar of chocolate – literally, from everywhere.

You can have so much fun choosing your colours; however, if you are not confident in choosing colours, a great way to find inspiration is to take a look at Pinterest or Google online. For example, if you search for pastel colour palettes it will show you some fantastic pastel colourways that you could then use as a starting point for a colour scheme for your blanket. You could also start by picking a theme, such as autumn or rainbow colours, and then search for inspiration online – the choices are endless!

For the blankets in this book, I chose to use lovely pastel shades with a few bright colours thrown in. Monochrome would also be fab and also maybe black and white. The only thing I would advise is to keep a neutral base colour. I have used cream and it works really well, but you could use a dark colour as your base, just as long as your pattern colours complement the base colour so that your illusion pops. See below for a few swatches of some possible colour schemes and examples of what results you might get if you were to choose a colourful base instead of a neutral one. You could even make your own swatches first to see what works best for your colourway.

Here are some samples that show how important it is to get the main colour right for your pattern. As you can see, a main colour that is too close in tone to the pattern colours doesn't look right and may distract from the illusion of the blanket itself.

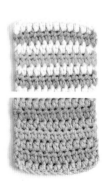

CHANGING COLOURS

Here I show you how to change colours while working your illusion blankets. The method is easy to follow and, once you get the hang of it, it will become second nature when following the patterns in this book – it might also be helpful for other crochet projects that have colour changes. There are two methods, changing colours right side facing and changing colours wrong side facing. The same method is used when adding a new colour.

CHANGING COLOURS (RS FACING)

Just before you finish the final stitch in the old colour, drop the yarn you are working with (here it is the cream) to the back of your blanket (A). Pick up the new colour on your hook (here it is purple) (B). Now pull through the three loops on your hook using the new colour (C). This completes the stitch in the old yarn and means you're ready to start the next stitch in the new colour. Keep all yarn to the back of your blanket when working on the RS.

CHANGING COLOURS (WS FACING)

Just before you finish the final stitch in the old colour, keeping the yarn to the front of the blanket, drop the yarn you are working with (here it is green) (D). Pick up the new colour on your hook (here it is cream) (E). Now pull through all three loops on your hook using the new colour (F). This completes the stitch in the old yarn and means you're ready to start the next stitch in the new colour. Keep all yarn to the front of your blanket when working on the WS.

RS FACING

WS FACING

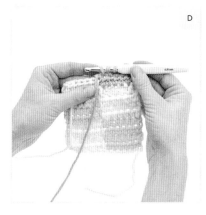
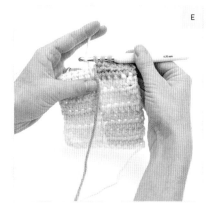
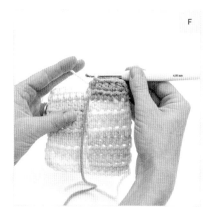

READING A CHART

Intarsia patterns are usually accompanied by charts, which are a brilliant visual aid you can use to keep your place as you work. When reading charts, always start at the bottom and work your way up to the top.

Each square of the chart represents one half double crochet stitch.

Read right side (odd-number) rows from right to left and wrong side (even-number) rows from left to right.

 Look out for this symbol, which indicates where charts have been rotated on the page.

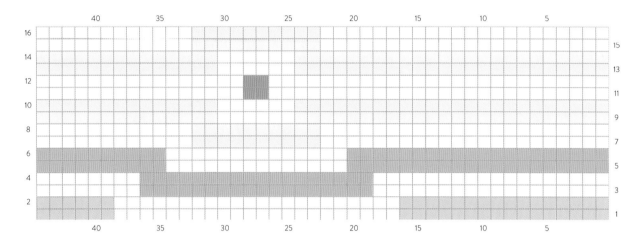

PATTERN NOTES

In this section, you will find all the notes you need for the patterns in the book.

TERMINOLOGY

The stitches used throughout the book are in US terms. The main stitch used is the hdc (half double crochet), which in UK terms is the htr (half treble crochet).

ABBREVIATIONS

The following abbreviations are used for the patterns in this book:

ch – chain

sl st – slip stitch

hdc – half double crochet

RS – right side facing

WS – wrong side facing

st(s) – stitch(es)

IMPORTANT NOTES

- Ch1 at the beginning of each row DOES NOT count as a stitch.
- Remember each square = 1 hdc stitch.
- Each row has the same number of stitches. The total number of stitches per row is indicated in just the first two rows.

TENSION (GAUGE)

Tension isn't important for the blanket projects in the book, and the yarn isn't carried under your stitches so no yarn will show through them. I have used aran (worsted) weight yarn throughout the book. If you were to use a different weight yarn – for example a DK (light worsted) weight yarn – then the resulting blanket will be smaller in size but the yarn weight won't affect the optical illusion of the blanket in any way.

WORKING INTARSIA CROCHET

This is probably the most important section for you to read through. The key to successful intarsia crochet is in managing your yarns; this is important because your yarn balls can easily get tangled up especially when using quite a few balls, as you do in these patterns. Here I explain the set up process and how to manage the yarn balls.

MANAGING YARNS

Each pattern in the book has a section called 'Yarn balls wound', which lists how many yarn balls of each colour you will need for the pattern, and what the weight of the yarn balls should be. The aim is to have enough yarn balls wound in each colour, so you don't need to wind any more during the blanket-making process. However, everybody's tension (gauge) is different, so it is possible that – even with the best preparation – you may need to wind a few more balls before the end of the pattern.

First, I set up my yarn winder and a set of kitchen scales on a table ready to wind my yarn. I then refer to the pattern I am going to make and wind all the yarn I need into the separate balls of yarn as specified in the Yarn Balls Wound list in the pattern, weighing the balls of yarn as I go (A).

For most of the blankets, the first couple of rows are the most complicated, so I try to get comfortable and have all the wound balls of yarn at hand ready to join them in. Once you have made your starting chain, it is on the first row that, for most of the patterns, you will start joining in yarn colours. As you join each yarn colour and the number of working yarn balls increases, you will find that you need something to hold the yarn balls when they are not in use but still attached to your blanket. I use a long basket to hold them to help prevent them from becoming tangled, but you can use anything that will hold the balls in a line (B).

Your yarn holder is now in front of you, you have finished your first row, and all the yarns are attached. To turn your work, flip your blanket over from left to right. This will result in the attached yarns crisscrossing over one another (C) – don't worry though, this is fine for the wrong side of your blanket and it will rectify itself on the next row.

TIP

As an alternative to winding small balls of yarn, you could use bobbins – small plastic or card frames that the yarn can be wound around.

While you work the next row – which is worked from the wrong side of the blanket – as you complete each colour, keep in mind that the colour that you are dropping needs to be dropped on the wrong side of the blanket. Do this for each change of colour along the row (D). Once you get to the end of the row, all the dropped yarns will be on the wrong side of the blanket (E).

Now, flip the blanket from left to right again and this will result in the attached yarns being at the back of your work and hopefully not tangled (F). Repeat this process as you follow the pattern.

So, you just need to remember that when you're working on the right side of the blanket, the attached yarns are at the back of the work, and when you're working on the wrong side of the blanket the attached yarns will come from under your work to the wrong side of the blanket. On the wrong side you must drop the yarns to the wrong side of your blanket, which will help prevent the yarns from getting tangled. However, please don't worry if this doesn't work first time – your yarns will probably get tangled at some point, but you can just lay your blanket down and sort them back into order.

RIGHT SIDE OR WRONG SIDE?

The difference between the right side and the wrong side of your blanket is important for yarn management. Not only this, but when changing colours, the yarn change is noticeable on the wrong side of your blanket and not noticeable at all on the right side of your blanket. See below for an example of the right and wrong side of a blanket.

RIGHT SIDE   WRONG SIDE

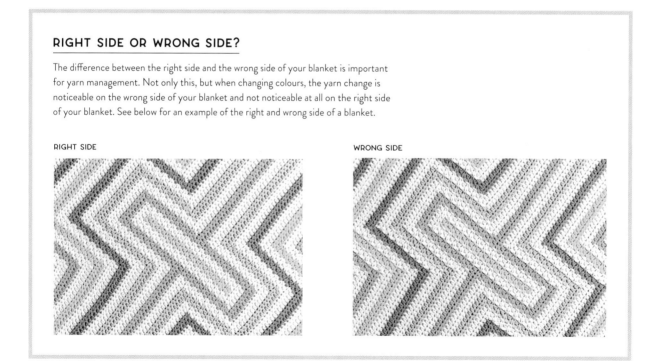

PICKING UP AND FASTENING OFF

Here, I show you where to pick up the yarn colours that are already joined in, and where to fasten them off. For the steps I am following the chart shown right.

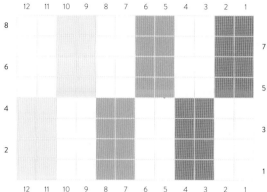

Here, you will see that I have followed the chart, completed Row 1, and turned my work ready to start Row 2. It's now time to pick up the yarns you have already attached and dropped at the wrong side of your blanket. Repeat across the row, picking up the dropped yarns as you go (G).

I have now finished Row 2 and you will see that I have dropped the yarns on the wrong side of the blanket at each colour change, following the chart (H). Turn your work and you're ready to start the next row (I). For Row 3, your yarns are now at the back of your blanket (wrong side) and after working the first two stitches, you need to pick up the pink from the back of your blanket (J). Continue following the chart and picking up the yarns needed and dropping them on the wrong side of the blanket to the end of Row 3 (K).

Now, turn your work and begin Row 4. You will notice on the chart that after Row 4, the colours and pattern change on the chart, which means it's time to start fastening colours off, ready to rejoin them on Row 5. After completing the first two stitches of Row 4 in the yellow, snip the yarn off, leaving a long enough yarn tail to sew in later (L). Continue to the end of the row, snipping the yarns off as you go.

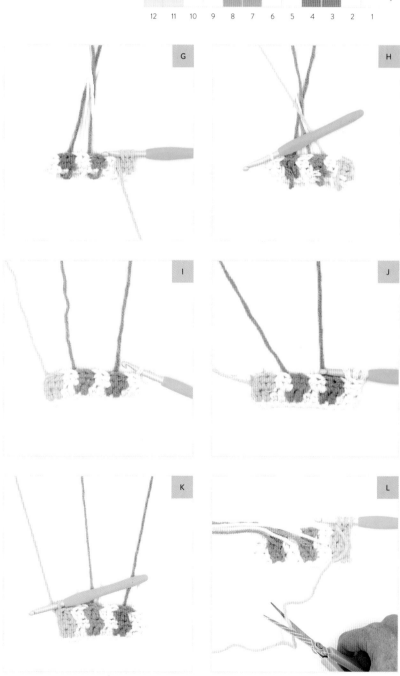

Now, join in the next colour at the start of Row 5 (M). Continue following the chart, completing the rows and reattaching yarns as you work until the pattern is complete (N).

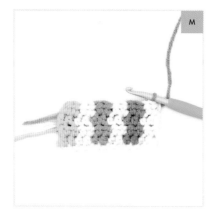

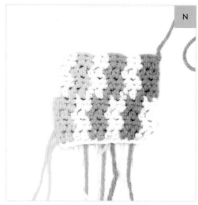

SEWING IN ENDS

Now let's tackle those yarn ends! Here you'll find step-by-step, illustrated instructions on how to sew in yarn ends using different methods to ensure those ends are secure and hidden neatly away. All sewing in of ends is done on the wrong side of the blanket and you should always try to sew your yarn ends into fabric of the same colour yarn, if possible.

METHOD 1

This method shows you how to sew in your colour-change yarn ends (A).

Thread the yarn end onto your yarn needle, and working on the same row as your end, thread your needle through the backs of the stitches in the same colour yarn as your tail (B). Pull the yarn end through, then thread it vertically through the back of several stitches on either the row above or below – again, in the same colour (C). Pull through, and then once again, thread through the backs of the stitches in the same colour yarn as your tail (D). Pull through, then snip off your end and that is your yarn tail sewn in. Repeat this process for all your colour changing yarn ends.

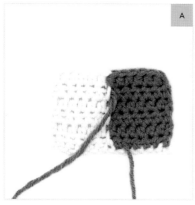

METHOD 2

This method demonstrates how to sew in the yarn ends from your starting chain.

Thread your yarn end onto your needle. Working on the same row as your end, take your needle and thread it through the backs of the stitches – if possible, in the same colour yarn as your tail. This example shows the yarn being threaded through a different colour – sometimes this is necessary, but as long as you thread carefully through the backs of your stitches (E) then it won't show at the front of your work. Pull the yarn through, and then thread the needle through the backs of more stitches along that row. Pull through, then snip off your end (F).

TIP

Try and sew in the yarn ends as you go. Intarsia crochet leaves a lot of ends to sew in (two for each colour change), so keeping on top of these as you work will help to keep your work neat and tidy and save you finishing time. You are most likely to have more ends to sew in at the beginning and end of your blanket.

METHOD 3

This method is for sewing in your last yarn tail once you have completed the blanket.

Thread your yarn end onto your needle and, on the same row as your end, take your needle and thread it through the backs of the stitches, if possible, in the same colour yarn as your tail (G). Pull through, then thread the needle vertically through the backs of a number of stitches on the rows below (H). Pull through and then thread your needle through the back of some stitches in the same colour yarn as your tail (I). Pull through and then snip off your yarn end (J).

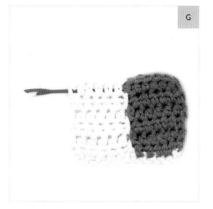

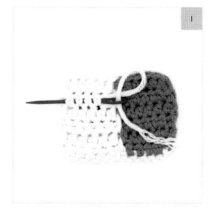

THE BLANKETS

CANDY
STRIPES

The soft pastel tones in this blanket design bring
to mind delicious candy, and the parallel bands
of colour radiate outwards, at the same time
creating two central interlocking diamonds.

YOU WILL NEED

HOOK

6.5mm (US K/10.5) hook

YARN

Scheepjes Truly Scrumptious (50% recycled polyester (recycled plastic bottles) and 50% acrylic), aran (worsted) weight, 100g (3½oz) = 108m (118yd), in the following shades:

- A: Buttercream Icing (302) x 6 balls
- B: Cotton Candy Meringue (330) x 2 balls
- E: Custard Pie (341) x 2 balls
- G: Mint Whoopie Pie (340) x 2 balls
- I: French Blue Macaron (343) x 2 balls

YARN BALLS WOUND

- A: 9 x 66g (2⅓oz)
- B: 3 x 66g (2⅓oz)
- E: 3 x 66g (2⅓oz)
- G: 3 x 66g (2⅓oz)
- I : 3 x 66g (2⅓oz)

TENSION (GAUGE)

11 stitches x 9 rows = 10cm (4in) square

FINISHED SIZE

122 x 90cm (48 x 35½in)

PATTERN

Using a 6.5mm (US K/10.5) hook, chain 97 in Yarn G. Now start in the 2nd chain from the hook.

Rows 1 and 2: (G) Ch1, 45hdc, (A) 2hdc, (E) 2hdc, (A) 2hdc, (G) 45hdc. (96 sts)

Rows 3 and 4: (A) Ch1, 43hdc, (G) 2hdc, (A) 2hdc, (E) 2hdc, (A) 2hdc, (G) 2hdc, (A) 43hdc.

Rows 5 and 6: (I) Ch1, 41hdc, (A) 2hdc, (G) 2hdc, (A) 2hdc, (E) 2hdc, (A) 2hdc, (G) 2hdc, (A) 2hdc, (I) 41hdc.

Rows 7 and 8: (A) Ch1, 39hdc, (I) 2hdc, (A) 2hdc, (G) 2hdc, (A) 2hdc, (E) 2hdc, (A) 2hdc, (G) 2hdc, (A) 2hdc, (I) 2hdc, (A) 39hdc.

Rows 9 and 10: (B) Ch1, 37hdc, (A) 2hdc, (I) 2hdc, (A) 2hdc, (G) 2hdc, (A) 2hdc, (E) 2hdc, (A) 2hdc, (G) 2hdc, (A) 2hdc, (I) 2hdc, (A) 2hdc, (B) 37hdc.

Rows 11 and 12: (A) Ch1, 35hdc, (B) 2hdc, (A) 2hdc, (I) 2hdc, (A) 2hdc, (G) 2hdc, (A) 2hdc, (E) 2hdc, (A) 2hdc, (G) 2hdc, (A) 2hdc, (I) 2hdc, (A) 2hdc, (B) 2hdc, (A) 35hdc.

Rows 13 and 14: (E) Ch1, 33hdc, (A) 2hdc, (B) 2hdc, (A) 2hdc, (I) 2hdc, (A) 2hdc, (G) 2hdc, (A) 2hdc, (E) 2hdc, (A) 2hdc, (G) 2hdc, (A) 2hdc, (I) 2hdc, (A) 2hdc, (B) 2hdc, (A) 2hdc, (E) 33hdc.

Rows 15 and 16: (A) Ch1, 31hdc, (E) 2hdc, (A) 2hdc, (B) 2hdc, (A) 2hdc, (I) 2hdc, (A) 2hdc, (G) 2hdc, (A) 6hdc, (G) 2hdc, (A) 2hdc, (I) 2hdc, (A) 2hdc, (B) 2hdc, (A) 2hdc, (E) 2hdc, (A) 31hdc.

Rows 17 and 18: (G) Ch1, 29hdc, (A) 2hdc, (E) 2hdc, (A) 2hdc, (B) 2hdc, (A) 2hdc, (I) 2hdc, (A) 2hdc, (G) 10hdc, (A) 2hdc, (I) 2hdc, (A) 2hdc, (B) 2hdc, (A) 2hdc, (E) 2hdc, (A) 2hdc, (G) 29hdc.

Rows 19 and 20: (A) Ch1, 27hdc, (G) 2hdc, (A) 2hdc, (E) 2hdc, (A) 2hdc, (B) 2hdc, (A) 2hdc, (I) 2hdc, (A) 14hdc, (I) 2hdc, (A) 2hdc, (B) 2hdc, (A) 2hdc, (E) 2hdc, (A) 2hdc, (G) 2hdc, (A) 27hdc.

Rows 21 and 22: (I) Ch1, 25hdc, (A) 2hdc, (G) 2hdc, (A) 2hdc, (E) 2hdc, (A) 2hdc, (B) 2hdc, (A) 2hdc, (I) 18hdc, (A) 2hdc, (B) 2hdc, (A) 2hdc, (E) 2hdc, (A) 2hdc, (G) 2hdc, (A) 2hdc, (I) 25hdc.

Rows 23 and 24: (A) Ch1, 23hdc, (I) 2hdc, (A) 2hdc, (G) 2hdc, (A) 2hdc, (E) 2hdc, (A) 2hdc, (B) 2hdc, (A) 22hdc, (B) 2hdc, (A) 2hdc, (E) 2hdc, (A) 2hdc, (G) 2hdc, (A) 2hdc, (I) 2hdc, (A) 23hdc.

Rows 25 and 26: (B) Ch1, 21hdc, (A) 2hdc, (I) 2hdc, (A) 2hdc, (G) 2hdc, (A) 2hdc, (E) 2hdc, (A) 2hdc, (B) 26hdc, (A) 2hdc, (E) 2hdc, (A) 2hdc, (G) 2hdc, (A) 2hdc, (I) 2hdc, (A) 2hdc, (B) 21hdc.

Rows 27 and 28: (A) Ch1, 19hdc, (B) 2hdc, (A) 2hdc, (I) 2hdc, (A) 2hdc, (G) 2hdc, (A) 2hdc, (E) 2hdc, (A) 30hdc, (E) 2hdc, (A) 2hdc, (G) 2hdc, (A) 2hdc, (I) 2hdc, (A) 2hdc, (B) 2hdc, (A) 19hdc.

Rows 29 and 30: (E) Ch1, 17hdc, (A) 2hdc, (B) 2hdc, (A) 2hdc, (I) 2hdc, (A) 2hdc, (G) 2hdc, (A) 2hdc, (E) 34hdc, (A) 2hdc, (G) 2hdc, (A) 2hdc, (I) 2hdc, (A) 2hdc, (B) 2hdc, (A) 2hdc, (E) 17hdc.

Rows 31 and 32: Repeat Rows 27 and 28.

Rows 33 and 34: Repeat Rows 25 and 26.

Rows 35 and 36: Repeat Rows 23 and 24.

Rows 37 and 38: Repeat Rows 21 and 22.

Rows 39 and 40: Repeat Rows 19 and 20.

Rows 41 and 42: Repeat Rows 17 and 18.

Rows 43 and 44: Repeat Rows 15 and 16.

Rows 45 and 46: Repeat Rows 13 and 14.

Rows 47 and 48: Repeat Rows 11 and 12.

Rows 49 and 50: Repeat Rows 9 and 10.

Rows 51 and 52: Repeat Rows 7 and 8.

Rows 53 and 54: Repeat Rows 5 and 6.

Rows 55 and 56: Repeat Rows 3 and 4.

Rows 57 to 112: Repeat Rows 1 to 56.

Rows 113 and 114: Repeat Rows 1 and 2.

Don't break yarn.

Row 115 (RS): (G) 96 sl sts across to the end.

Fasten off, and sew in all yarn ends.

Add tassels or pompoms if desired.

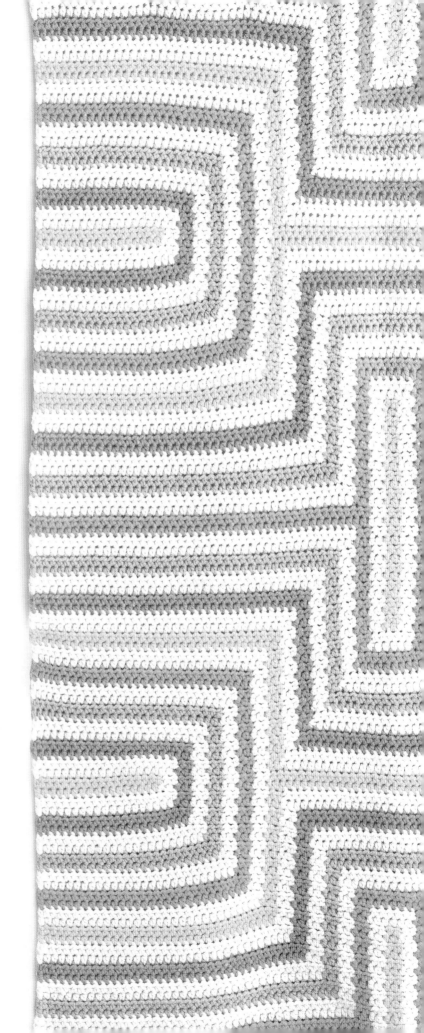

WORKING FROM CHART

For each row, work all stitches from 1 to 96. Work Rows 1 to 56 twice, then repeat Rows 1 and 2 once more. Continue with Row 115 of written instructions.

Continue with Row 115 of written instructions.

TIPS

Don't forget, 1 square on the chart = 1 hdc stitch!

Take your time to get familiar with the chart before starting your blanket.

KEY

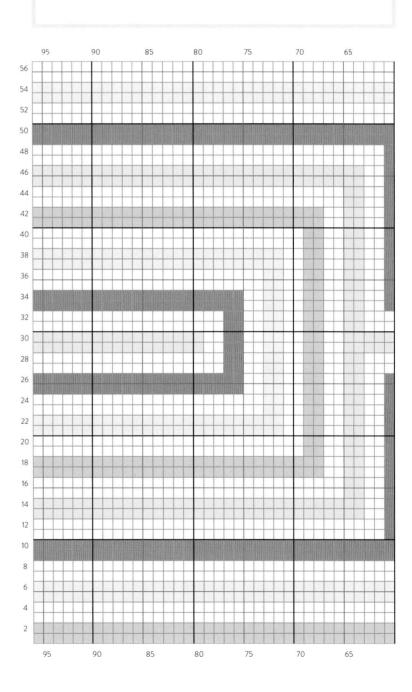

☐ Buttercream Icing

▓ Cotton Candy Meringue

▓ Custard Pie

▓ Mint Whoopie Pie

▓ French Blue Macaron

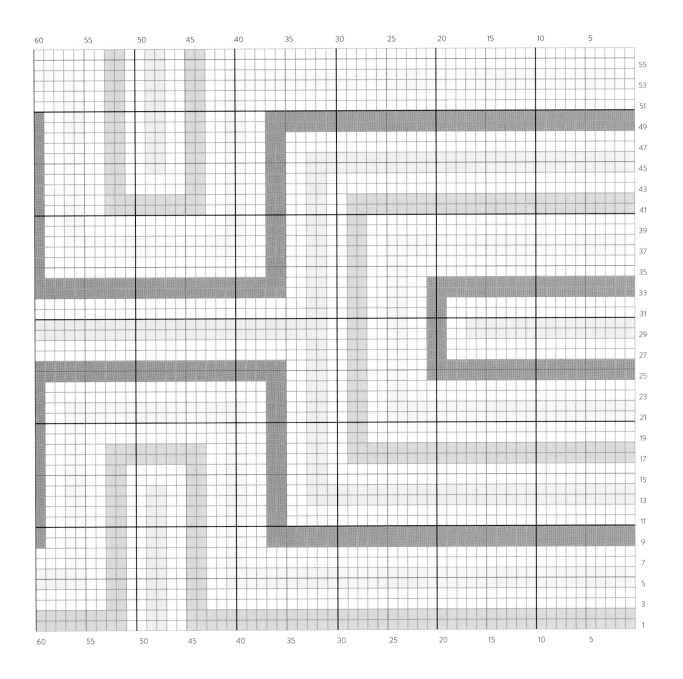

PURPLE
HAZE

The warm tones of purple, pink, orange and yellow in this blanket design seem to pulse, while breaking the squares along two vertical lines creates a three-dimensional optical illusion.

YOU WILL NEED

HOOK

6.5mm (US K/10.5) hook

YARN

Scheepjes Truly Scrumptious (50% recycled polyester (recycled plastic bottles) and 50% acrylic), aran (worsted) weight, 100g (3½oz) = 108m (118yd), in the following shades:

- A: Buttercream Icing (302) x 6 balls
- C: Rose Barfi (321) x 2 balls
- D: Orange Cheesecake (332) x 1 ball
- E: Custard Pie (341) x 1 ball
- K: Sweet Potato Mochi (320) x 3 balls

YARN BALLS WOUND

- A: 25 x 24g (⅞oz)
- C: 6 x 33g (1⅙oz)
- D: 4 x 25g (⅞oz)
- E: 4 x 25g (⅞oz)
- K: 10 x 30g (1oz)

TENSION (GAUGE)

11 stitches x 9 rows = 10cm (4in) square

FINISHED SIZE

112 x 85cm (44 x 33½in)

PATTERN

Using a 6.5mm (US K/10.5) hook, chain 99 in Yarn A. Now start in the 2nd chain from the hook.

Rows 1 and 2: (A) Ch1, 2hdc, (C) 2hdc, (A) 2hdc, (K) 2hdc, (A) 2hdc, (K) 2hdc, (A) 2hdc, (K) 2hdc, (A) 2hdc, (C) 2hdc, (A) 2hdc, (D) 2hdc, (A) 2hdc, (E) 2hdc, (A) 2hdc, (K) 2hdc, (A) 2hdc, (E) 2hdc, (A) 2hdc, (D) 2hdc, (A) 2hdc, (C) 2hdc, (A) 2hdc, (K) 2hdc, (A) 2hdc, (K) 2hdc, (A) 2hdc, (C) 2hdc, (A) 2hdc, (D) 2hdc, (A) 2hdc, (E) 2hdc, (A) 2hdc, (K) 2hdc, (A) 2hdc, (E) 2hdc, (A) 2hdc, (D) 2hdc, (A) 2hdc, (C) 2hdc, (A) 2hdc, (K) 2hdc, (A) 2hdc, (K) 2hdc, (A) 2hdc, (K) 2hdc, (A) 2hdc, (C) 2hdc, (A) 2hdc. (98 sts)

Rows 3 and 4: (A) Ch1, 2hdc, (C) 2hdc, (A) 2hdc, (K) 2hdc, (A) 2hdc, (K) 2hdc, (A) 2hdc, (K) 2hdc, (A) 2hdc, (C) 2hdc, (A) 2hdc, (D) 2hdc, (A) 2hdc, (E) 4hdc, (A) 4hdc, (E) 2hdc, (A) 2hdc, (D) 2hdc, (A) 2hdc, (C) 2hdc, (A) 2hdc, (K) 2hdc, (A) 2hdc, (K) 2hdc, (A) 2hdc, (C) 2hdc, (A) 2hdc, (D) 2hdc, (A) 2hdc, (E) 2hdc, (A) 4hdc, (E) 4hdc, (A) 2hdc, (D) 2hdc, (A) 2hdc, (C) 2hdc, (A) 2hdc, (K) 2hdc, (A) 2hdc, (K) 2hdc, (A) 2hdc, (K) 2hdc, (A) 2hdc, (C) 2hdc, (A) 2hdc.

Rows 5 and 6: (A) Ch1, 2hdc, (C) 2hdc, (A) 2hdc, (K) 2hdc, (A) 2hdc, (K) 2hdc, (A) 2hdc, (K) 2hdc, (A) 2hdc, (C) 2hdc, (A) 2hdc, (D) 2hdc, (A) 6hdc, (E) 6hdc, (A) 2hdc, (D) 2hdc, (A) 2hdc, (C) 2hdc, (A) 2hdc, (K) 2hdc, (A) 2hdc, (K) 2hdc, (A) 2hdc, (C) 2hdc, (A) 2hdc, (D) 2hdc, (A) 2hdc, (E) 6hdc, (A) 6hdc, (D) 2hdc, (A) 2hdc, (C) 2hdc, (A) 2hdc, (K) 2hdc, (A) 2hdc, (K) 2hdc, (A) 2hdc, (K) 2hdc, (A) 2hdc, (C) 2hdc, (A) 2hdc.

Rows 7 and 8: (A) Ch1, 2hdc, (C) 2hdc, (A) 2hdc, (K) 2hdc, (A) 2hdc, (K) 2hdc, (A) 2hdc, (K) 2hdc, (A) 2hdc, (C) 2hdc, (A) 2hdc, (D) 8hdc, (A) 8hdc, (D) 2hdc, (A) 2hdc, (C) 2hdc, (A) 2hdc, (K) 2hdc, (A) 2hdc, (K) 2hdc, (A) 2hdc, (C) 2hdc, (A) 2hdc, (D) 2hdc, (A) 8hdc, (D) 8hdc, (A) 2hdc, (C) 2hdc, (A) 2hdc, (K) 2hdc, (A) 2hdc, (K) 2hdc, (A) 2hdc, (K) 2hdc, (A) 2hdc, (C) 2hdc, (A) 2hdc.

Rows 9 and 10: (A) Ch1, 2hdc, (C) 2hdc, (A) 2hdc, (K) 2hdc, (A) 2hdc, (K) 2hdc, (A) 2hdc, (K) 2hdc, (A) 2hdc, (C) 2hdc, (A) 10hdc, (D) 10hdc, (A) 2hdc, (C) 2hdc, (A) 2hdc, (K) 2hdc, (A) 2hdc, (K) 2hdc, (A) 2hdc, (C) 2hdc, (A) 2hdc, (D) 10hdc, (A) 10hdc, (C) 2hdc, (A) 2hdc, (K) 2hdc, (A) 2hdc, (K) 2hdc, (A) 2hdc, (K) 2hdc, (A) 2hdc, (C) 2hdc, (A) 2hdc.

Rows 11 and 12: (C) Ch1, 4hdc, (A) 2hdc, (K) 2hdc, (A) 2hdc, (K) 2hdc, (A) 2hdc, (K) 2hdc, (A) 2hdc, (C) 12hdc, (A) 12hdc, (C) 2hdc, (A) 2hdc, (K) 2hdc, (A) 2hdc, (K) 2hdc, (A) 2hdc, (C) 2hdc, (A) 12hdc, (C) 12hdc, (A) 2hdc, (K) 2hdc, (A) 2hdc, (K) 2hdc, (A) 2hdc, (K) 2hdc, (A) 2hdc, (C) 4hdc.

Rows 13 and 14: (A) Ch1, 6hdc, (K) 2hdc, (A) 2hdc, (K) 2hdc, (A) 2hdc, (K) 2hdc, (A) 14hdc, (C) 14hdc, (A) 2hdc, (K) 2hdc, (A) 2hdc, (K) 2hdc, (A) 2hdc, (C) 14hdc, (A) 14hdc, (K) 2hdc, (A) 2hdc, (K) 2hdc, (A) 2hdc, (K) 2hdc, (A) 6hdc.

Rows 15 and 16: (K) Ch1, 8hdc, (A) 2hdc, (K) 2hdc, (A) 2hdc, (K) 16hdc, (A) 16hdc, (K) 2hdc, (A) 2hdc, (K) 2hdc, (A) 16hdc, (K) 16hdc, (A) 2hdc, (K) 2hdc, (A) 2hdc, (K) 8hdc.

Rows 17 and 18: (A) Ch1, 10hdc, (K) 2hdc, (A) 18hdc, (K) 18hdc, (A) 2hdc, (K) 18hdc, (A) 18hdc, (K) 2hdc, (A) 10hdc.

Rows 19 and 20: (K) Ch1, 30hdc, (A) 38hdc, (K) 30hdc.

Rows 21 and 22: (A) Ch1, 10hdc, (K) 2hdc, (A) 18hdc, (K) 18hdc, (A) 2hdc, (K) 18hdc, (A) 18hdc, (K) 2hdc, (A) 10hdc.

Rows 23 and 24: (K) Ch1, 8hdc, (A) 2hdc, (K) 2hdc, (A) 2hdc, (K) 16hdc, (A) 16hdc, (K) 2hdc, (A) 2hdc, (K) 2hdc, (A) 16hdc, (K) 16hdc, (A) 2hdc, (K) 2hdc, (A) 2hdc, (K) 8hdc.

Rows 25 and 26: (A) Ch1, 6hdc, (K) 2hdc, (A) 2hdc, (K) 2hdc, (A) 2hdc, (K) 2hdc, (A) 14hdc, (C) 14hdc, (A) 2hdc, (K) 2hdc, (A) 2hdc, (K) 2hdc, (A) 2hdc, (C) 14hdc, (A) 14hdc, (K) 2hdc, (A) 2hdc, (K) 2hdc, (A) 2hdc, (K) 2hdc, (A) 6hdc.

Rows 27 and 28: (C) Ch1, 4hdc, (A) 2hdc, (K) 2hdc, (A) 2hdc, (K) 2hdc, (A) 2hdc, (K) 2hdc, (A) 2hdc, (C) 12hdc, (A) 12hdc, (C) 2hdc, (A) 2hdc, (K) 2hdc, (A) 2hdc, (K) 2hdc, (A) 2hdc, (C) 2hdc, (A) 12hdc, (C) 12hdc, (A) 2hdc, (K) 2hdc, (A) 2hdc, (K) 2hdc, (A) 2hdc, (K) 2hdc, (A) 2hdc, (C) 4hdc.

Rows 29 and 30: (A) Ch1, 2hdc, (C) 2hdc, (A) 2hdc, (K) 2hdc, (A) 2hdc, (K) 2hdc, (A) 2hdc, (K) 2hdc, (A) 2hdc, (C) 2hdc, (A) 10hdc, (D) 10hdc, (A) 2hdc, (C) 2hdc, (A) 2hdc, (K) 2hdc, (A) 2hdc, (K) 2hdc, (A) 2hdc, (C) 2hdc, (A) 2hdc, (D) 10hdc, (A) 10hdc, (C) 2hdc, (A) 2hdc, (K) 2hdc, (A) 2hdc, (K) 2hdc, (A) 2hdc, (K) 2hdc, (A) 2hdc, (C) 2hdc, (A) 2hdc.

Rows 31 and 32: (A) Ch1, 2hdc, (C) 2hdc, (A) 2hdc, (K) 2hdc, (A) 2hdc, (K) 2hdc, (A) 2hdc, (K) 2hdc, (A) 2hdc, (C) 2hdc, (A) 2hdc, (D) 8hdc, (A) 8hdc, (D) 2hdc, (A) 2hdc, (C) 2hdc, (A) 2hdc, (K) 2hdc, (A) 2hdc, (K) 2hdc, (A) 2hdc, (C) 2hdc, (A) 2hdc, (D) 2hdc, (A) 8hdc, (D) 8hdc, (A) 2hdc, (C) 2hdc, (A) 2hdc, (K) 2hdc, (A) 2hdc, (K) 2hdc, (A) 2hdc, (K) 2hdc, (A) 2hdc, (C) 2hdc, (A) 2hdc.

Rows 33 and 34: (A) Ch1, 2hdc, (C) 2hdc, (A) 2hdc, (K) 2hdc, (A) 2hdc, (K) 2hdc, (A) 2hdc, (K) 2hdc, (A) 2hdc, (C) 2hdc, (A) 2hdc, (D) 2hdc, (A) 6hdc, (E) 6hdc, (A) 2hdc, (D) 2hdc, (A) 2hdc, (C) 2hdc, (A) 2hdc, (K) 2hdc, (A) 2hdc, (K) 2hdc, (A) 2hdc, (C) 2hdc, (A) 2hdc, (D) 2hdc, (A) 2hdc, (E) 6hdc, (A) 6hdc, (D) 2hdc, (A) 2hdc, (C) 2hdc, (A) 2hdc, (K) 2hdc, (A) 2hdc, (K) 2hdc, (A) 2hdc, (K) 2hdc, (A) 2hdc, (C) 2hdc, (A) 2hdc.

Rows 35 and 36: (A) Ch1, 2hdc, (C) 2hdc, (A) 2hdc, (K) 2hdc, (A) 2hdc, (K) 2hdc, (A) 2hdc, (K) 2hdc, (A) 2hdc, (C) 2hdc, (A) 2hdc, (D) 2hdc, (A) 2hdc, (E) 4hdc, (A) 4hdc, (E) 2hdc, (A) 2hdc, (D) 2hdc, (A) 2hdc, (C) 2hdc, (A) 2hdc, (K) 2hdc, (A) 2hdc, (K) 2hdc, (A) 2hdc, (C) 2hdc, (A) 2hdc, (D) 2hdc, (A) 2hdc, (E) 2hdc, (A) 4hdc, (E) 4hdc, (A) 2hdc, (D) 2hdc, (A) 2hdc, (C) 2hdc, (A) 2hdc, (K) 2hdc, (A) 2hdc, (K) 2hdc, (A) 2hdc, (K) 2hdc, (A) 2hdc, (C) 2hdc, (A) 2hdc.

Rows 37 to 72: Repeat Rows 1 to 36.

Rows 73 to 108: Repeat Rows 1 to 36.

Rows 109 and 110: Repeat Rows 1 and 2.

Don't break yarn.

Row 111 (RS): (A) 98 sl sts across to the end.

Fasten off, and sew in all yarn ends.

Add tassels or pompoms if desired.

WORKING FROM CHART

For each row, work all stitches from 1 to 99. Work Rows 1 to 36 three times, then work Rows 1 and 2 once more. Continue with Row 111 of written instructions.

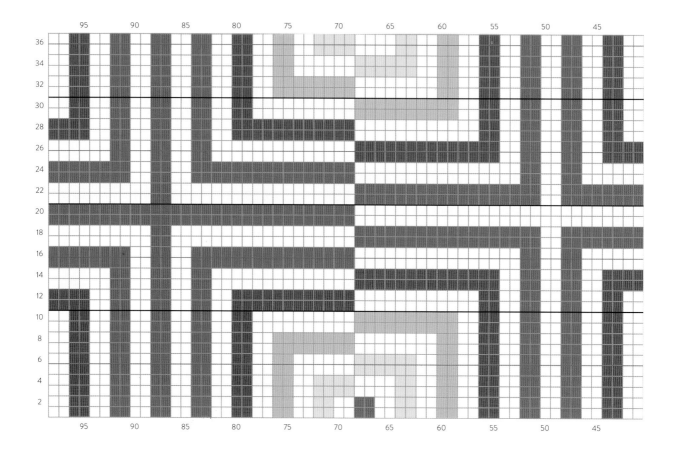

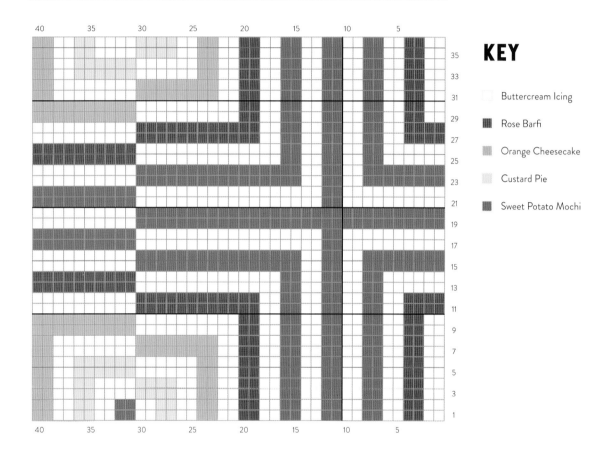

KEY

Buttercream Icing

Rose Barfi

Orange Cheesecake

Custard Pie

Sweet Potato Mochi

RIPPLE EFFECT

The stripes and zigzags that radiate outwards from the central square of this blanket appear to ripple and move as you gaze at them. The toning colours add to the effect, but it would work as well in darker shades.

YOU WILL NEED

HOOK

6.5mm (US K/10.5) hook

YARN

Scheepjes Truly Scrumptious (50% recycled polyester (recycled plastic bottles) and 50% acrylic), aran (worsted) weight, 100g (3½oz) = 108m (118yd), in the following shades:

- A: Buttercream Icing (302) x 6 balls
- E: Custard Pie (341) x 1 ball
- G: Mint Whoopie Pie (340) x 2 balls
- J: Lavender Slice (334) x 2 balls

YARN BALLS WOUND

- A: 20 x 30g (1oz)
- E: 6 x 33g (1⅙oz)
- G: 8 x 25g (⅞oz)
- J: 7 x 28g (1oz)

TENSION (GAUGE)

11 stitches x 9 rows = 10cm (4in) square

FINISHED SIZE

112 x 87cm (44 x 34in)

PATTERN

Using a 6.5mm (US K/10.5) hook, chain 99 in Yarn G. Now start in the 2nd chain from the hook.

Rows 1 and 2: (G) Ch1, 10hdc, (A) 2hdc, (J) 2hdc, (A) 2hdc, (E) 2hdc, (A) 2hdc, (G) 2hdc, (A) 2hdc, (J) 2hdc, (A) 2hdc, (E) 2hdc, (A) 2hdc, (G) 2hdc, (A) 2hdc, (J) 2hdc, (A) 2hdc, (E) 2hdc, (A) 2hdc, (G) 2hdc, (A) 2hdc, (J) 2hdc, (A) 2hdc, (G) 2hdc, (A) 2hdc, (E) 2hdc, (A) 2hdc, (J) 2hdc, (A) 2hdc, (G) 2hdc, (A) 2hdc, (E) 2hdc, (A) 2hdc, (J) 2hdc, (A) 2hdc, (G) 2hdc, (A) 2hdc, (E) 2hdc, (A) 2hdc, (J) 2hdc, (A) 2hdc, (G) 10hdc. (98 sts)

Rows 3 and 4: (A) Ch1, 12hdc, (J) 2hdc, (A) 2hdc, (E) 2hdc, (A) 2hdc, (G) 2hdc, (A) 2hdc, (J) 2hdc, (A) 2hdc, (E) 2hdc, (A) 2hdc, (G) 2hdc, (A) 2hdc, (J) 2hdc, (A) 2hdc, (E) 2hdc, (A) 2hdc, (G) 2hdc, (A) 2hdc, (J) 2hdc, (A) 2hdc, (G) 2hdc, (A) 2hdc, (E) 2hdc, (A) 2hdc, (J) 2hdc, (A) 2hdc, (G) 2hdc, (A) 2hdc, (E) 2hdc, (A) 2hdc, (J) 2hdc, (A) 2hdc, (G) 2hdc, (A) 2hdc, (E) 2hdc, (A) 2hdc, (J) 2hdc, (A) 12hdc.

Rows 5 and 6: (J) Ch1, 14hdc, (A) 2hdc, (E) 2hdc, (A) 2hdc, (G) 2hdc, (A) 2hdc, (J) 2hdc, (A) 2hdc, (E) 2hdc, (A) 2hdc, (G) 2hdc, (A) 2hdc, (J) 2hdc, (A) 2hdc, (E) 2hdc, (A) 2hdc, (G) 2hdc, (A) 2hdc, (J) 2hdc, (A) 2hdc, (G) 2hdc, (A) 2hdc, (E) 2hdc, (A) 2hdc, (J) 2hdc, (A) 2hdc, (G) 2hdc, (A) 2hdc, (E) 2hdc, (A) 2hdc, (J) 2hdc, (A) 2hdc, (G) 2hdc, (A) 2hdc, (E) 2hdc, (A) 2hdc, (J) 14hdc.

Rows 7 and 8: (A) Ch1, 16hdc, (E) 2hdc, (A) 2hdc, (G) 2hdc, (A) 2hdc, (J) 2hdc, (A) 2hdc, (E) 2hdc, (A) 2hdc, (G) 2hdc, (A) 2hdc, (J) 2hdc, (A) 2hdc, (E) 2hdc, (A) 2hdc, (G) 2hdc, (A) 2hdc, (J) 2hdc, (A) 2hdc, (G) 2hdc, (A) 2hdc, (E) 2hdc, (A) 2hdc, (J) 2hdc, (A) 2hdc, (G) 2hdc, (A) 2hdc, (E) 2hdc, (A) 2hdc, (J) 2hdc, (A) 2hdc, (G) 2hdc, (A) 2hdc, (E) 2hdc, (A) 16hdc.

Rows 9 and 10: (E) Ch1, 18hdc, (A) 2hdc, (G) 2hdc, (A) 2hdc, (J) 2hdc, (A) 2hdc, (E) 2hdc, (A) 2hdc, (G) 2hdc, (A) 2hdc, (J) 2hdc, (A) 2hdc, (E) 2hdc, (A) 2hdc, (G) 2hdc, (A) 2hdc, (J) 2hdc, (A) 2hdc, (G) 2hdc, (A) 2hdc, (E) 2hdc, (A) 2hdc, (J) 2hdc, (A) 2hdc, (G) 2hdc, (A) 2hdc, (E) 2hdc, (A) 2hdc, (J) 2hdc, (A) 2hdc, (G) 2hdc, (A) 2hdc, (E) 18hdc.

Rows 11 and 12: (E) Ch1, 2hdc, (A) 18hdc, (G) 2hdc, (A) 2hdc, (J) 2hdc, (A) 2hdc, (E) 2hdc, (A) 2hdc, (G) 2hdc, (A) 2hdc, (J) 2hdc, (A) 2hdc, (E) 2hdc, (A) 2hdc, (G) 2hdc, (A) 2hdc, (J) 2hdc, (A) 2hdc, (G) 2hdc, (A) 2hdc, (E) 2hdc, (A) 2hdc, (J) 2hdc, (A) 2hdc, (G) 2hdc, (A) 2hdc, (E) 2hdc, (A) 2hdc, (J) 2hdc, (A) 2hdc, (G) 2hdc, (A) 18hdc, (E) 2hdc.

Rows 13 and 14: (E) Ch1, 2hdc, (A) 2hdc, (G) 18hdc, (A) 2hdc, (J) 2hdc, (A) 2hdc, (E) 2hdc, (A) 2hdc, (G) 2hdc, (A) 2hdc, (J) 2hdc, (A) 2hdc, (E) 2hdc, (A) 2hdc, (G) 2hdc, (A) 2hdc, (J) 2hdc, (A) 2hdc, (G) 2hdc, (A) 2hdc, (E) 2hdc, (A) 2hdc, (J) 2hdc, (A) 2hdc, (G) 2hdc, (A) 2hdc, (E) 2hdc, (A) 2hdc, (J) 2hdc, (A) 2hdc, (G) 18hdc, (A) 2hdc, (E) 2hdc.

Rows 15 and 16: (E) Ch1, 2hdc, (A) 2hdc, (G) 2hdc, (A) 18hdc, (J) 2hdc, (A) 2hdc, (E) 2hdc, (A) 2hdc, (G) 2hdc, (A) 2hdc, (J) 2hdc, (A) 2hdc, (E) 2hdc, (A) 2hdc, (G) 2hdc, (A) 2hdc, (J) 2hdc, (A) 2hdc, (G) 2hdc, (A) 2hdc, (E) 2hdc, (A) 2hdc, (J) 2hdc, (A) 2hdc, (G) 2hdc, (A) 2hdc, (E) 2hdc, (A) 2hdc, (J) 2hdc, (A) 18hdc, (G) 2hdc, (A) 2hdc, (E) 2hdc.

Rows 17 and 18: (E) Ch1, 2hdc, (A) 2hdc, (G) 2hdc, (A) 2hdc, (J) 18hdc, (A) 2hdc, (E) 2hdc, (A) 2hdc, (G) 2hdc, (A) 2hdc, (J) 2hdc, (A) 2hdc, (E) 2hdc, (A) 2hdc, (G) 2hdc, (A) 2hdc, (J) 2hdc, (A) 2hdc, (G) 2hdc, (A) 2hdc, (E) 2hdc, (A) 2hdc, (J) 2hdc, (A) 2hdc, (G) 2hdc, (A) 2hdc, (E) 2hdc, (A) 2hdc, (J) 18hdc, (A) 2hdc, (G) 2hdc, (A) 2hdc, (E) 2hdc.

Rows 19 and 20: (E) Ch1, 2hdc, (A) 2hdc, (G) 2hdc, (A) 2hdc, (J) 2hdc, (A) 18hdc, (E) 2hdc, (A) 2hdc, (G) 2hdc, (A) 2hdc, (J) 2hdc, (A) 2hdc, (E) 2hdc, (A) 2hdc, (G) 2hdc, (A) 2hdc, (J) 2hdc, (A) 2hdc, (G) 2hdc, (A) 2hdc, (E) 2hdc, (A) 2hdc, (J) 2hdc, (A) 2hdc, (G) 2hdc, (A) 2hdc, (E) 2hdc, (A) 18hdc, (J) 2hdc, (A) 2hdc, (G) 2hdc, (A) 2hdc, (E) 2hdc.

Rows 21 and 22: (A) Ch1, 4hdc, (G) 2hdc, (A) 2hdc, (J) 2hdc, (A) 2hdc, (E) 18hdc, (A) 2hdc, (G) 2hdc, (A) 2hdc, (J) 2hdc, (A) 2hdc, (E) 2hdc, (A) 2hdc, (G) 2hdc, (A) 2hdc, (J) 2hdc, (A) 2hdc, (G) 2hdc, (A) 2hdc, (E) 2hdc, (A) 2hdc, (J) 2hdc, (A) 2hdc, (G) 2hdc, (A) 2hdc, (E) 18hdc, (A) 2hdc, (J) 2hdc, (A) 2hdc, (G) 2hdc, (A) 4hdc.

Rows 23 and 24: (G) Ch1, 6hdc, (A) 2hdc, (J) 2hdc, (A) 2hdc, (E) 2hdc, (A) 18hdc, (G) 2hdc, (A) 2hdc, (J) 2hdc, (A) 2hdc, (E) 2hdc, (A) 2hdc, (G) 2hdc, (A) 2hdc, (J) 2hdc, (A) 2hdc, (G) 2hdc, (A) 2hdc, (E) 2hdc, (A) 2hdc, (J) 2hdc, (A) 2hdc, (G) 2hdc, (A) 18hdc, (E) 2hdc, (A) 2hdc, (J) 2hdc, (A) 2hdc, (G) 6hdc.

Rows 25 and 26: (A) Ch1, 8hdc, (J) 2hdc, (A) 2hdc, (E) 2hdc, (A) 2hdc, (G) 18hdc, (A) 2hdc, (J) 2hdc, (A) 2hdc, (E) 2hdc, (A) 2hdc, (G) 2hdc, (A) 2hdc, (J) 2hdc, (A) 2hdc, (G) 2hdc, (A) 2hdc, (E) 2hdc, (A) 2hdc, (J) 2hdc, (A) 2hdc, (G) 18hdc, (A) 2hdc, (E) 2hdc, (A) 2hdc, (J) 2hdc, (A) 8hdc.

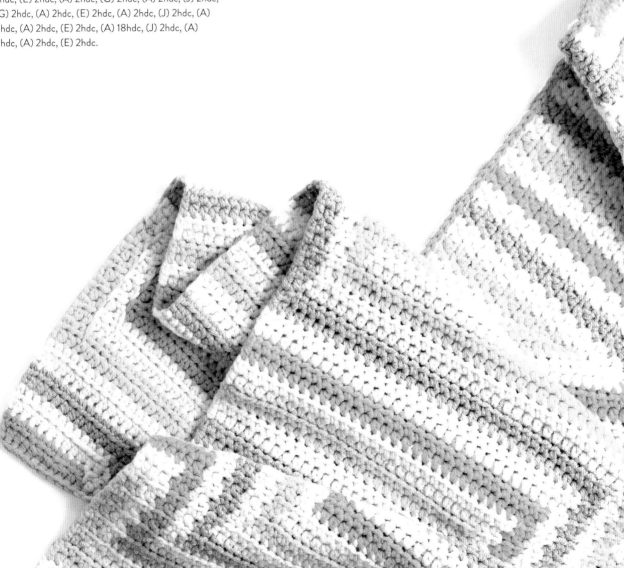

Rows 27 and 28: (J) Ch1, 10hdc, (A) 2hdc, (E) 2hdc, (A) 2hdc, (G) 2hdc, (A) 18hdc, (J) 2hdc, (A) 2hdc, (E) 2hdc, (A) 2hdc, (G) 2hdc, (A) 2hdc, (J) 2hdc, (A) 2hdc, (G) 2hdc, (A) 2hdc, (E) 2hdc, (A) 2hdc, (J) 2hdc, (A) 18hdc, (G) 2hdc, (A) 2hdc, (E) 2hdc, (A) 2hdc, (J) 10hdc.

Rows 29 and 30: (A) Ch1, 12hdc, (E) 2hdc, (A) 2hdc, (G) 2hdc, (A) 2hdc, (J) 18hdc, (A) 2hdc, (E) 2hdc, (A) 2hdc, (G) 2hdc, (A) 2hdc, (J) 2hdc, (A) 2hdc, (G) 2hdc, (A) 2hdc, (E) 2hdc, (A) 2hdc, (J) 18hdc, (A) 2hdc, (G) 2hdc, (A) 2hdc, (E) 2hdc, (A) 12hdc.

Rows 31 and 32: (E) Ch1, 14hdc, (A) 2hdc, (G) 2hdc, (A) 2hdc, (J) 2hdc, (A) 18hdc, (E) 2hdc, (A) 2hdc, (G) 2hdc, (A) 2hdc, (J) 2hdc, (A) 2hdc, (G) 2hdc, (A) 2hdc, (E) 2hdc, (A) 18hdc, (J) 2hdc, (A) 2hdc, (G) 2hdc, (A) 2hdc, (E) 14hdc.

Rows 33 and 34: (A) Ch1, 16hdc, (G) 2hdc, (A) 2hdc, (J) 2hdc, (A) 2hdc, (E) 18hdc, (A) 2hdc, (G) 2hdc, (A) 2hdc, (J) 2hdc, (A) 2hdc, (G) 2hdc, (A) 2hdc, (E) 18hdc, (A) 2hdc, (J) 2hdc, (A) 2hdc, (G) 2hdc, (A) 16hdc.

Rows 35 and 36: (G) Ch1, 18hdc, (A) 2hdc, (J) 2hdc, (A) 2hdc, (E) 2hdc, (A) 18hdc, (G) 2hdc, (A) 2hdc, (J) 2hdc, (A) 2hdc, (G) 2hdc, (A) 18hdc, (E) 2hdc, (A) 2hdc, (J) 2hdc, (A) 2hdc, (G) 18hdc.

Rows 37 and 38: (A) Ch1, 20hdc, (J) 2hdc, (A) 2hdc, (E) 2hdc, (A) 2hdc, (G) 18hdc, (A) 2hdc, (J) 2hdc, (A) 2hdc, (G) 18hdc, (A) 2hdc, (E) 2hdc, (A) 2hdc, (J) 2hdc, (A) 20hdc.

Rows 39 and 40: (J) Ch1, 22hdc, (A) 2hdc, (E) 2hdc, (A) 2hdc, (G) 2hdc, (A) 18hdc, (J) 2hdc, (A) 18hdc, (G) 2hdc, (A) 2hdc, (E) 2hdc, (A) 2hdc, (J) 22hdc.

Rows 41 and 42: (A) Ch1, 24hdc, (E) 2hdc, (A) 2hdc, (G) 2hdc, (A) 2hdc, (J) 34hdc, (A) 2hdc, (G) 2hdc, (A) 2hdc, (E) 2hdc, (A) 24hdc.

Rows 43 and 44: (E) Ch1, 26hdc, (A) 2hdc, (G) 2hdc, (A) 2hdc, (J) 2hdc, (A) 30hdc, (J) 2hdc, (A) 2hdc, (G) 2hdc, (A) 2hdc, (E) 26hdc.

Rows 45 and 46: (A) Ch1, 28hdc, (G) 2hdc, (A) 2hdc, (J) 2hdc, (A) 2hdc, (E) 26hdc, (A) 2hdc, (J) 2hdc, (A) 2hdc, (G) 2hdc, (A) 28hdc.

Rows 47 and 48: (G) Ch1, 30hdc, (A) 2hdc, (J) 2hdc, (A) 2hdc, (E) 2hdc, (A) 22hdc, (E) 2hdc, (A) 2hdc, (J) 2hdc, (A) 2hdc, (G) 30hdc.

Rows 49 and 50: (A) Ch1, 32hdc, (J) 2hdc, (A) 2hdc, (E) 2hdc, (A) 2hdc, (G) 18hdc, (A) 2hdc, (E) 2hdc, (A) 2hdc, (J) 2hdc, (A) 32hdc.

Rows 51 and 52: (J) Ch1, 34hdc, (A) 2hdc, (E) 2hdc, (A) 2hdc, (G) 2hdc, (A) 14hdc, (G) 2hdc, (A) 2hdc, (E) 2hdc, (A) 2hdc, (J) 34hdc.

Rows 53 and 54: (J) Ch1, 2hdc, (A) 34hdc, (E) 2hdc, (A) 2hdc, (G) 2hdc, (A) 2hdc, (J) 10hdc, (A) 2hdc, (G) 2hdc, (A) 2hdc, (E) 2hdc, (A) 34hdc, (J) 2hdc.

Rows 55 and 56: (J) Ch1, 2hdc, (A) 2hdc, (E) 34hdc, (A) 2hdc, (G) 2hdc, (A) 2hdc, (J) 2hdc, (A) 6hdc, (J) 2hdc, (A) 2hdc, (G) 2hdc, (A) 2hdc, (E) 34hdc, (A) 2hdc, (J) 2hdc.

Rows 57 and 58: (J) Ch1, 2hdc, (A) 2hdc, (E) 2hdc, (A) 34hdc, (G) 2hdc, (A) 2hdc, (J) 2hdc, (A) 2hdc, (E) 2hdc, (A) 2hdc, (J) 2hdc, (A) 2hdc, (G) 2hdc, (A) 34hdc, (E) 2hdc, (A) 2hdc, (J) 2hdc.

TIP

As you work your blanket, snip off and remove any unused yarn balls from your basket to help keep everything tidy. See Working Intarsia Crochet: Managing Yarns for more information.

Rows 59 and 60: Repeat Rows 55 and 56.

Rows 61 and 62: Repeat Rows 53 and 54.

Rows 63 and 64: Repeat Rows 51 and 52.

Rows 65 and 66: Repeat Rows 49 and 50.

Rows 67 and 68: Repeat Rows 47 and 48.

Rows 69 and 70: Repeat Rows 45 and 46.

Rows 71 and 72: Repeat Rows 43 and 44.

Rows 73 and 74: Repeat Rows 41 and 42.

Rows 75 and 76: Repeat Rows 39 and 40.

Rows 77 and 78: Repeat Rows 37 and 38.

Rows 79 and 80: Repeat Rows 35 and 36.

Rows 81 and 82: Repeat Rows 33 and 34.

Rows 83 and 84: Repeat Rows 31 and 32.

Rows 85 and 86: Repeat Rows 29 and 30.

Rows 87 and 88: Repeat Rows 27 and 28.

Rows 89 and 90: Repeat Rows 25 and 26.

Rows 91 and 92: Repeat Rows 23 and 24.

Rows 93 and 94: Repeat Rows 21 and 22.

Rows 95 and 96: Repeat Rows 19 and 20.

Rows 97 and 98: Repeat Rows 17 and 18.

Rows 99 and 100: Repeat Rows 15 and 16.

Rows 101 and 102: Repeat Rows 13 and 14.

Rows 103 and 104: Repeat Rows 11 and 12.

Rows 105 and 106: Repeat Rows 9 and 10.

Rows 107 and 108: Repeat Rows 7 and 8.

Rows 109 and 110: Repeat Rows 5 and 6.

Rows 111 and 112: Repeat Rows 3 and 4.

Rows 113 and 114: Repeat Rows 1 and 2.

Don't break yarn.

Row 115 (RS): (G) 98 sl sts across to the end.

Fasten off, and sew in all yarn ends.

Add tassels or pompoms if desired.

WORKING FROM CHART

For each row, work all stitches from 1 to 98.
Work Rows 1 to 114 once. Continue with
Row 115 of written instructions.

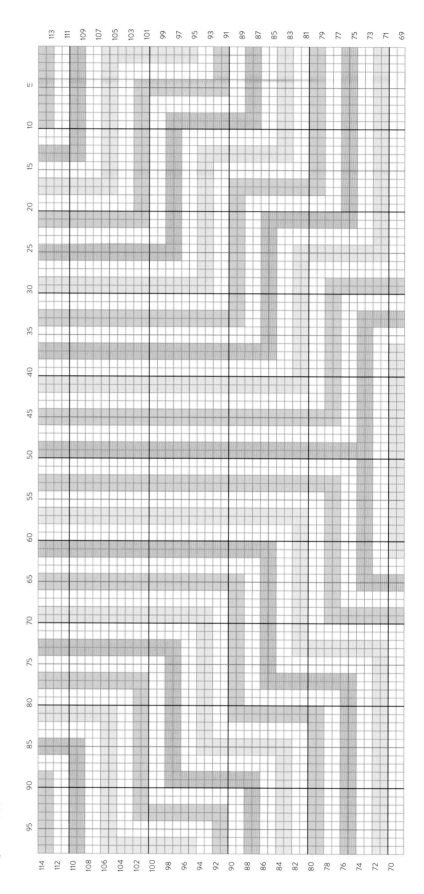

KEY

- ☐ Buttercream Icing
- ▦ Custard Pie
- ▦ Mint Whoopie Pie
- ▦ Lavender Slice

FLOATING
DIAMONDS

The contours of the stripes that flow across this blanket design are reminiscent of ripples on the surface of water. The offset lines create multiple diamond shapes in a geometric grid.

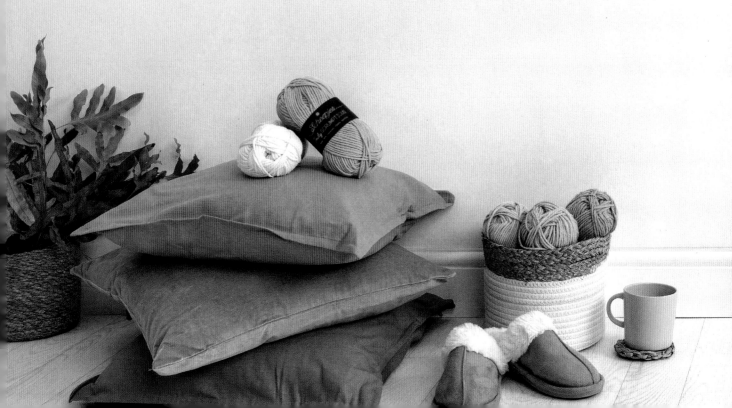

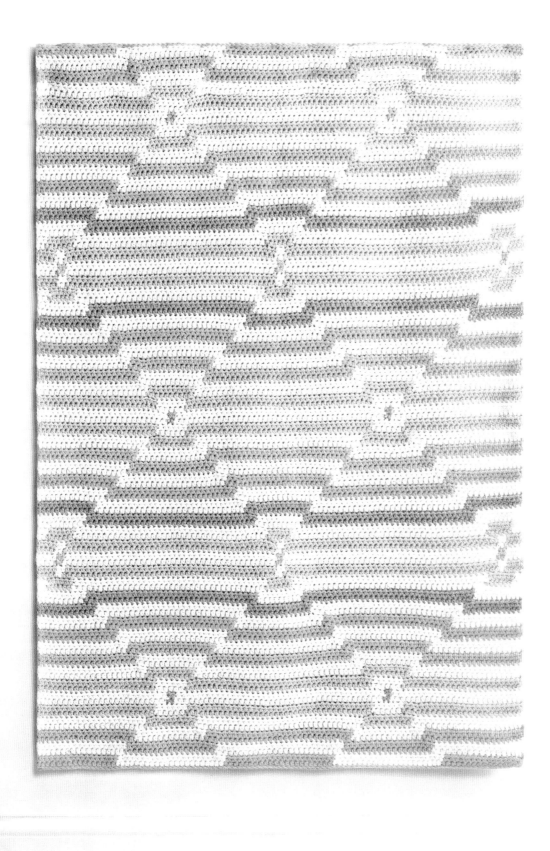

YOU WILL NEED

HOOK

6.5mm (US K/10.5) hook

YARN

Scheepjes Truly Scrumptious (50% recycled polyester (recycled plastic bottles) and 50% acrylic), aran (worsted) weight, 100g (3½oz) = 108m (118yd), in the following shades:

- A: Buttercream Icing (302) x 5 balls
- B: Cotton Candy Meringue (330) x 1 ball
- D: Orange Cheesecake (332) x 2 balls
- G: Mint Whoopie Pie (340) x 2 balls
- I: French Blue Macaron (343) x 2 balls

YARN BALLS WOUND

- A: 4 x 125g (4½oz)
- B: 3 x 33g (1⅛oz)
- D: 3 x 66g (2⅓oz)
- G: 3 x 66g (2⅓oz)
- I: 4 x 50g (1¾oz)

TENSION (GAUGE)

11 stitches x 9 rows = 10cm (4in) square

FINISHED SIZE

119 x 87cm (47 x 34in)

PATTERN

Using a 6.5mm (US K/10.5) hook, chain 99 in Yarn G. Now start in the 2nd chain from the hook.

Rows 1 and 2: (G) Ch1, 16hdc, (A) 22hdc, (G) 22hdc, (A) 22hdc, (G) 16hdc. (98 sts)

Rows 3 and 4: (A) Ch1, 18hdc, (D) 18hdc, (A) 26hdc, (D) 18hdc, (A) 18hdc.

Rows 5 and 6: (D) Ch1, 20hdc, (A) 14hdc, (D) 30hdc, (A) 14hdc, (D) 20hdc.

Rows 7 and 8: (A) Ch1, 22hdc, (I) 10hdc, (A) 34hdc, (I) 10hdc, (A) 22hdc.

Rows 9 and 10: (I) Ch1, 24hdc, (A) 6hdc, (I) 38hdc, (A) 6hdc, (I) 24hdc.

Rows 11 and 12: (A) Ch1, 26hdc, (B) 2hdc, (A) 42hdc, (B) 2hdc, (A) 26hdc.

Rows 13 and 14: (I) Ch1, 24hdc, (A) 6hdc, (I) 38hdc, (A) 6hdc, (I) 24hdc.

Rows 15 and 16: (A) Ch1, 22hdc, (I) 10hdc, (A) 34hdc, (I) 10hdc, (A) 22hdc.

Rows 17 and 18: (D) Ch1, 20hdc, (A) 14hdc, (D) 30hdc, (A) 14hdc, (D) 20hdc.

Rows 19 and 20: (A) Ch1, 18hdc, (D) 18hdc, (A) 26hdc, (D) 18hdc, (A) 18hdc.

Rows 21 and 22: (G) Ch1, 16hdc, (A) 22hdc, (G) 22hdc, (A) 22hdc, (G) 16hdc.

Rows 23 and 24: (A) Ch1, 14hdc, (G) 26hdc, (A) 18hdc, (G) 26hdc, (A) 14hdc.

Rows 25 and 26: (B) Ch1, 12hdc, (A) 30hdc, (B) 14hdc, (A) 30hdc, (B) 12hdc.

Rows 27 and 28: (A) Ch1, 10hdc, (B) 34hdc, (A) 10hdc, (B) 34hdc, (A) 10hdc.

Rows 29 and 30: (A) Ch1, 2hdc, (I) 6hdc, (A) 38hdc, (I) 6hdc, (A) 38hdc, (I) 6hdc, (A) 2hdc.

Rows 31 and 32: (I) Ch1, 4hdc, (A) 2hdc, (I) 42hdc, (A) 2hdc, (I) 42hdc, (A) 2hdc, (I) 4hdc.

Rows 33 and 34: (A) Ch1, 4hdc, (D) 2hdc, (A) 42hdc, (D) 2hdc, (A) 42hdc, (D) 2hdc, (A) 4hdc.

Rows 35 and 36: (I) Ch1, 4hdc, (A) 2hdc, (I) 42hdc, (A) 2hdc, (I) 42hdc, (A) 2hdc, (I) 4hdc.

Rows 37 and 38: (A) Ch1, 2hdc, (I) 6hdc, (A) 38hdc, (I) 6hdc, (A) 38hdc, (I) 6hdc, (A) 2hdc.

Rows 39 and 40: (A) Ch1, 10hdc, (B) 34hdc, (A) 10hdc, (B) 34hdc, (A) 10hdc.

Rows 41 and 42: (B) Ch1, 12hdc, (A) 30hdc, (B) 14hdc, (A) 30hdc, (B) 12hdc.

Rows 43 and 44: (A) Ch1, 14hdc, (G) 26hdc, (A) 18hdc, (G) 26hdc, (A) 14hdc.

Rows 45 to 88: Repeat rows 1 to 44.

Rows 89 to 110: Repeat rows 1 to 22.

Don't break yarn.

Row 111 (RS): (G) 98 sl sts across to the end.

Fasten off, and sew in all yarn ends.

Add tassels or pompoms if desired.

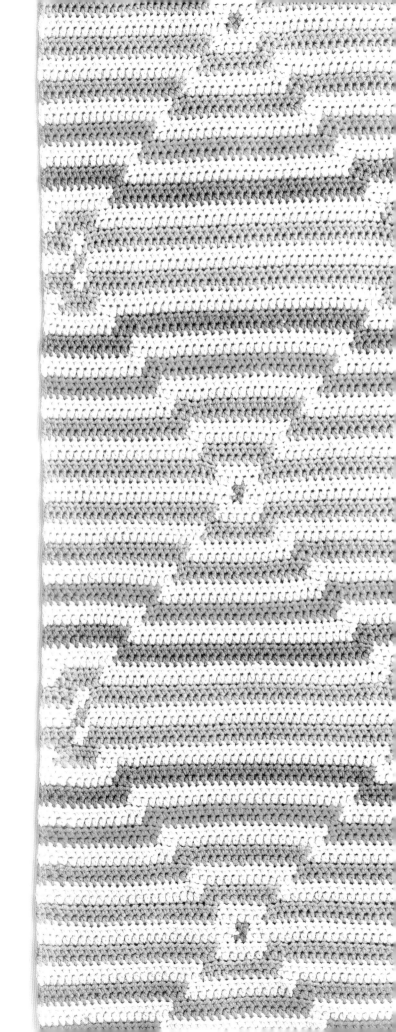

WORKING FROM CHART

For each row, work all stitches from 1 to 98. Work
Rows 1 to 44 twice, then work Rows 1 to 22 once more.
Continue with Row 111 of written instructions.

KEY

☐ Buttercream Icing

▦ Cotton Candy Meringue

▦ Orange Cheesecake

▦ Mint Whoopie Pie

▦ French Blue Macaron

TIP

When working on the right side of your
blanket, the chart will read from right to
left. When working on the wrong side of
your blanket, the chart will read from left to
right. See Working Intarsia Crochet: Right
Side or Wrong Side? for how to identify
which side you are working on.

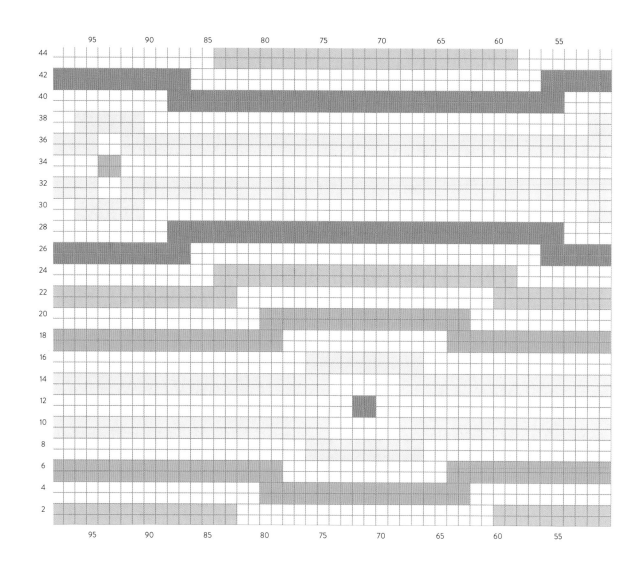

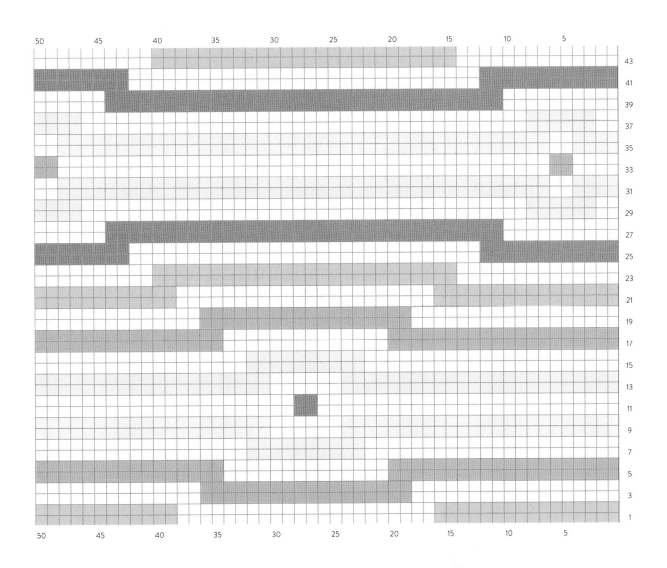

PASTEL
PYRAMIDS

This pattern seems to reveal a pyramid seen from above, formed from bands of pink, peach and mint stripes. But look again and it might be a curved tunnel receding into the distance.

YOU WILL NEED

HOOK

6.5mm (US K/10.5) hook

YARN

Scheepjes Truly Scrumptious (50% recycled polyester (recycled plastic bottles) and 50% acrylic), aran (worsted) weight, 100g (3½oz) = 108m (118yd), in the following shades:

- A: Buttercream Icing (302) x 6 balls
- B: Cotton Candy Meringue (330) x 2 balls
- D: Orange Cheesecake (332) x 2 balls
- F: Pistachio Bundt Cake (318) x 3 balls

YARN BALLS WOUND

- A: 25 x 24g (⅞oz)
- B: 8 x 25g (⅞oz)
- D: 8 x 25g (⅞oz)
- F: 8 x 37g (1¼oz)

TENSION (GAUGE)

11 stitches x 9 rows = 10cm (4in) square

FINISHED SIZE

121 x 90cm (47½ x 35½in)

PATTERN

Using a 6.5mm (US K/10.5) hook, chain 101 in Yarn A. Now start in the 2nd chain from the hook.

Rows 1 and 2: (A) Ch1, 2hdc, (F) 2hdc, (A) 2hdc, (D) 2hdc, (A) 2hdc, (B) 18hdc, (A) 2hdc, (F) 40hdc, (A) 2hdc, (B) 18hdc, (A) 2hdc, (D) 2hdc, (A) 2hdc, (F) 2hdc, (A) 2hdc. (100 sts)

Rows 3 and 4: (A) Ch1, 2hdc, (F) 2hdc, (A) 2hdc, (D) 2hdc, (A) 2hdc, (B) 2hdc, (A) 18hdc, (F) 40hdc, (A) 18hdc, (B) 2hdc, (A) 2hdc, (D) 2hdc, (A) 2hdc, (F) 2hdc, (A) 2hdc.

Rows 5 and 6: (A) Ch1, 2hdc, (F) 2hdc, (A) 2hdc, (D) 2hdc, (A) 2hdc, (B) 2hdc, (A) 18hdc, (F) 2hdc, (A) 36hdc, (F) 2hdc, (A) 18hdc, (B) 2hdc, (A) 2hdc, (D) 2hdc, (A) 2hdc, (F) 2hdc, (A) 2hdc.

Rows 7 and 8: (A) Ch1, 2hdc, (F) 2hdc, (A) 2hdc, (D) 2hdc, (A) 2hdc, (B) 2hdc, (A) 2hdc, (F) 18hdc, (A) 36hdc, (F) 18hdc, (A) 2hdc, (B) 2hdc, (A) 2hdc, (D) 2hdc, (A) 2hdc, (F) 2hdc, (A) 2hdc.

Rows 9 and 10: (A) Ch1, 2hdc, (F) 2hdc, (A) 2hdc, (D) 2hdc, (A) 2hdc, (B) 2hdc, (A) 2hdc, (F) 18hdc, (A) 2hdc, (D) 32hdc, (A) 2hdc, (F) 18hdc, (A) 2hdc, (B) 2hdc, (A) 2hdc, (D) 2hdc, (A) 2hdc, (F) 2hdc, (A) 2hdc.

Rows 11 and 12: (A) Ch1, 2hdc, (F) 2hdc, (A) 2hdc, (D) 2hdc, (A) 2hdc, (B) 2hdc, (A) 2hdc, (F) 2hdc, (A) 18hdc, (D) 32hdc, (A) 18hdc, (F) 2hdc, (A) 2hdc, (B) 2hdc, (A) 2hdc, (D) 2hdc, (A) 2hdc, (F) 2hdc, (A) 2hdc.

Rows 13 and 14: (A) Ch1, 2hdc, (F) 2hdc, (A) 2hdc, (D) 2hdc, (A) 2hdc, (B) 2hdc, (A) 2hdc, (F) 2hdc, (A) 18hdc, (D) 2hdc, (A) 28hdc, (D) 2hdc, (A) 18hdc, (F) 2hdc, (A) 2hdc, (B) 2hdc, (A) 2hdc, (D) 2hdc, (A) 2hdc, (F) 2hdc, (A) 2hdc.

Rows 15 and 16: (A) Ch1, 2hdc, (F) 2hdc, (A) 2hdc, (D) 2hdc, (A) 2hdc, (B) 2hdc, (A) 2hdc, (F) 2hdc, (A) 2hdc, (D) 18hdc, (A) 28hdc, (D) 18hdc, (A) 2hdc, (F) 2hdc, (A) 2hdc, (B) 2hdc, (A) 2hdc, (D) 2hdc, (A) 2hdc, (F) 2hdc, (A) 2hdc.

Rows 17 and 18: (A) Ch1, 2hdc, (F) 2hdc, (A) 2hdc, (D) 2hdc, (A) 2hdc, (B) 2hdc, (A) 2hdc, (F) 2hdc, (A) 2hdc, (D) 18hdc, (A) 2hdc, (B) 24hdc, (A) 2hdc, (D) 18hdc, (A) 2hdc, (F) 2hdc, (A) 2hdc, (B) 2hdc, (A) 2hdc, (D) 2hdc, (A) 2hdc, (F) 2hdc, (A) 2hdc.

Rows 19 and 20: (A) Ch1, 2hdc, (F) 2hdc, (A) 2hdc, (D) 2hdc, (A) 2hdc, (B) 2hdc, (A) 2hdc, (F) 2hdc, (A) 2hdc, (D) 2hdc, (A) 18hdc, (B) 24hdc, (A) 18hdc, (D) 2hdc, (A) 2hdc, (F) 2hdc, (A) 2hdc, (B) 2hdc, (A) 2hdc, (D) 2hdc, (A) 2hdc, (F) 2hdc, (A) 2hdc.

Rows 21 and 22: (A) Ch1, 2hdc, (F) 2hdc, (A) 2hdc, (D) 2hdc, (A) 2hdc, (B) 2hdc, (A) 2hdc, (F) 2hdc, (A) 2hdc, (D) 2hdc, (A) 18hdc, (B) 2hdc, (A) 20hdc, (B) 2hdc, (A) 18hdc, (D) 2hdc, (A) 2hdc, (F) 2hdc, (A) 2hdc, (B) 2hdc, (A) 2hdc, (D) 2hdc, (A) 2hdc, (F) 2hdc, (A) 2hdc.

Rows 23 and 24: (A) Ch1, 2hdc, (F) 2hdc, (A) 2hdc, (D) 2hdc, (A) 2hdc, (B) 2hdc, (A) 2hdc, (F) 2hdc, (A) 2hdc, (D) 2hdc, (A) 2hdc, (B) 18hdc, (A) 20hdc, (B) 18hdc, (A) 2hdc, (D) 2hdc, (A) 2hdc, (F) 2hdc, (A) 2hdc, (B) 2hdc, (A) 2hdc, (D) 2hdc, (A) 2hdc, (F) 2hdc, (A) 2hdc.

Rows 25 and 26: (A) Ch1, 2hdc, (F) 2hdc, (A) 2hdc, (D) 2hdc, (A) 2hdc, (B) 2hdc, (A) 2hdc, (F) 2hdc, (A) 2hdc, (D) 2hdc, (A) 2hdc, (B) 18hdc, (A) 2hdc, (F) 16hdc, (A) 2hdc, (B) 18hdc, (A) 2hdc, (D) 2hdc, (A) 2hdc, (F) 2hdc, (A) 2hdc, (B) 2hdc, (A) 2hdc, (D) 2hdc, (A) 2hdc, (F) 2hdc, (A) 2hdc.

Rows 27 and 28: (A) Ch1, 2hdc, (F) 2hdc, (A) 2hdc, (D) 2hdc, (A) 2hdc, (B) 2hdc, (A) 2hdc, (F) 2hdc, (A) 2hdc, (D) 2hdc, (A) 2hdc, (B) 2hdc, (A) 18hdc, (F) 16hdc, (A) 18hdc, (B) 2hdc, (A) 2hdc, (D) 2hdc, (A) 2hdc, (F) 2hdc, (A) 2hdc, (B) 2hdc, (A) 2hdc, (D) 2hdc, (A) 2hdc, (F) 2hdc, (A) 2hdc.

Rows 29 and 30: (A) Ch1, 2hdc, (F) 2hdc, (A) 2hdc, (D) 2hdc, (A) 2hdc, (B) 2hdc, (A) 2hdc, (F) 2hdc, (A) 2hdc, (D) 2hdc, (A) 2hdc, (B) 2hdc, (A) 18hdc, (F) 2hdc, (A) 12hdc, (F) 2hdc, (A) 18hdc, (B) 2hdc, (A) 2hdc, (D) 2hdc, (A) 2hdc, (F) 2hdc, (A) 2hdc, (B) 2hdc, (A) 2hdc, (D) 2hdc, (A) 2hdc, (F) 2hdc, (A) 2hdc.

Rows 31 and 32: (A) Ch1, 2hdc, (F) 2hdc, (A) 2hdc, (D) 2hdc, (A) 2hdc, (B) 2hdc, (A) 2hdc, (F) 2hdc, (A) 2hdc, (D) 2hdc, (A) 2hdc, (B) 2hdc, (A) 2hdc, (F) 18hdc, (A) 12hdc, (F) 18hdc, (A) 2hdc, (B) 2hdc, (A) 2hdc, (D) 2hdc, (A) 2hdc, (F) 2hdc, (A) 2hdc, (B) 2hdc, (A) 2hdc, (D) 2hdc, (A) 2hdc, (F) 2hdc, (A) 2hdc.

Rows 33 and 34: (A) Ch1, 2hdc, (F) 2hdc, (A) 2hdc, (D) 2hdc, (A) 2hdc, (B) 2hdc, (A) 2hdc, (F) 2hdc, (A) 2hdc, (D) 2hdc, (A) 2hdc, (B) 2hdc, (A) 2hdc, (F) 18hdc, (A) 2hdc, (D) 8hdc, (A) 2hdc, (F) 18hdc, (A) 2hdc, (B) 2hdc, (A) 2hdc, (D) 2hdc, (A) 2hdc, (F) 2hdc, (A) 2hdc, (B) 2hdc, (A) 2hdc, (D) 2hdc, (A) 2hdc, (F) 2hdc, (A) 2hdc.

Rows 35 and 36: (A) Ch1, 2hdc, (F) 2hdc, (A) 2hdc, (D) 2hdc, (A) 2hdc, (B) 2hdc, (A) 2hdc, (F) 2hdc, (A) 2hdc, (D) 2hdc, (A) 2hdc, (B) 2hdc, (A) 2hdc, (F) 2hdc, (A) 18hdc, (D) 8hdc, (A) 18hdc, (F) 2hdc, (A) 2hdc, (B) 2hdc, (A) 2hdc, (D) 2hdc, (A) 2hdc, (F) 2hdc, (A) 2hdc, (B) 2hdc, (A) 2hdc, (D) 2hdc, (A) 2hdc, (F) 2hdc, (A) 2hdc.

Rows 37 and 38: (A) Ch1, 2hdc, (F) 2hdc, (A) 2hdc, (D) 2hdc, (A) 2hdc, (B) 2hdc, (A) 2hdc, (F) 2hdc, (A) 2hdc, (D) 2hdc, (A) 2hdc, (B) 2hdc, (A) 2hdc, (F) 2hdc, (A) 18hdc, (D) 2hdc, (A) 4hdc, (D) 2hdc, (A) 18hdc, (F) 2hdc, (A) 2hdc, (B) 2hdc, (A) 2hdc, (D) 2hdc, (A) 2hdc, (F) 2hdc, (A) 2hdc.

Rows 39 and 40: (A) Ch1, 2hdc, (F) 2hdc, (A) 2hdc, (D) 2hdc, (A) 2hdc, (B) 2hdc, (A) 2hdc, (F) 2hdc, (A) 2hdc, (D) 2hdc, (A) 2hdc, (B) 2hdc, (A) 2hdc, (F) 2hdc, (A) 2hdc, (D) 18hdc, (A) 4hdc, (D) 18hdc, (A) 2hdc, (F) 2hdc, (A) 2hdc, (B) 2hdc, (A) 2hdc, (D) 2hdc, (A) 2hdc, (F) 2hdc, (A) 2hdc, (B) 2hdc, (A) 2hdc, (D) 2hdc, (A) 2hdc, (F) 2hdc, (A) 2hdc.

Rows 41 and 42: (A) Ch1, 2hdc, (F) 2hdc, (A) 2hdc, (D) 2hdc, (A) 2hdc, (B) 2hdc, (A) 2hdc, (F) 2hdc, (A) 2hdc, (D) 2hdc, (A) 2hdc, (B) 2hdc, (A) 2hdc, (F) 2hdc, (A) 2hdc, (D) 2hdc, (A) 36hdc, (D) 2hdc, (A) 2hdc, (F) 2hdc, (A) 2hdc, (B) 2hdc, (A) 2hdc, (D) 2hdc, (A) 2hdc, (F) 2hdc, (A) 2hdc, (B) 2hdc, (A) 2hdc, (D) 2hdc, (A) 2hdc, (F) 2hdc, (A) 2hdc.

Rows 43 and 44: (A) Ch1, 2hdc, (F) 2hdc, (A) 2hdc, (D) 2hdc, (A) 2hdc, (B) 2hdc, (A) 2hdc, (F) 2hdc, (A) 2hdc, (D) 2hdc, (A) 2hdc, (B) 2hdc, (A) 2hdc, (F) 2hdc, (A) 2hdc, (D) 2hdc, (A) 2hdc, (B) 32hdc, (A) 2hdc, (D) 2hdc, (A) 2hdc, (F) 2hdc, (A) 2hdc, (B) 2hdc, (A) 2hdc, (D) 2hdc, (A) 2hdc, (F) 2hdc, (A) 2hdc, (B) 2hdc, (A) 2hdc, (D) 2hdc, (A) 2hdc, (F) 2hdc, (A) 2hdc.

Rows 45 and 46: (A) Ch1, 2hdc, (F) 2hdc, (A) 2hdc, (D) 2hdc, (A) 2hdc, (B) 2hdc, (A) 2hdc, (F) 2hdc, (A) 2hdc, (D) 2hdc, (A) 2hdc, (B) 2hdc, (A) 2hdc, (F) 2hdc, (A) 2hdc, (D) 2hdc, (A) 2hdc, (B) 28hdc, (B) 2hdc, (A) 2hdc, (D) 2hdc, (A) 2hdc, (F) 2hdc, (A) 2hdc, (B) 2hdc, (A) 2hdc, (D) 2hdc, (A) 2hdc, (F) 2hdc, (A) 2hdc, (B) 2hdc, (A) 2hdc, (D) 2hdc, (A) 2hdc, (F) 2hdc, (A) 2hdc.

Rows 47 and 48: (A) Ch1, 2hdc, (F) 2hdc, (A) 2hdc, (D) 2hdc, (A) 2hdc, (B) 2hdc, (A) 2hdc, (F) 2hdc, (A) 2hdc, (D) 2hdc, (A) 2hdc, (B) 2hdc, (A) 2hdc, (F) 2hdc, (A) 2hdc, (D) 2hdc, (A) 2hdc, (B) 2hdc, (A) 2hdc, (F) 24hdc, (A) 2hdc, (B) 2hdc, (A) 2hdc, (D) 2hdc, (A) 2hdc, (F) 2hdc, (A) 2hdc, (B) 2hdc, (A) 2hdc, (D) 2hdc, (A) 2hdc, (F) 2hdc, (A) 2hdc, (B) 2hdc, (A) 2hdc, (D) 2hdc, (A) 2hdc, (F) 2hdc, (A) 2hdc.

Rows 49 and 50: (A) Ch1, 2hdc, (F) 2hdc, (A) 2hdc, (D) 2hdc, (A) 2hdc, (B) 2hdc, (A) 2hdc, (F) 2hdc, (A) 2hdc, (D) 2hdc, (A) 2hdc, (B) 2hdc, (A) 2hdc, (F) 2hdc, (A) 20hdc, (F) 2hdc, (A) 2hdc, (B) 2hdc, (A) 2hdc, (D) 2hdc, (A) 2hdc, (F) 2hdc, (A) 2hdc, (B) 2hdc, (A) 2hdc, (D) 2hdc, (A) 2hdc, (F) 2hdc, (A) 2hdc, (B) 2hdc, (A) 2hdc, (D) 2hdc, (A) 2hdc, (F) 2hdc, (A) 2hdc.

Rows 51 and 52: (A) Ch1, 2hdc, (F) 2hdc, (A) 2hdc, (D) 2hdc, (A) 2hdc, (B) 2hdc, (A) 2hdc, (F) 2hdc, (A) 2hdc, (D) 2hdc, (A) 2hdc, (B) 2hdc, (A) 2hdc, (F) 2hdc, (A) 2hdc, (D) 16hdc, (A) 2hdc, (F) 2hdc, (A) 2hdc, (B) 2hdc, (A) 2hdc, (D) 2hdc, (A) 2hdc, (F) 2hdc, (A) 2hdc, (B) 2hdc, (A) 2hdc, (D) 2hdc, (A) 2hdc, (F) 2hdc, (A) 2hdc, (B) 2hdc, (A) 2hdc, (D) 2hdc, (A) 2hdc, (F) 2hdc, (A) 2hdc.

Rows 53 and 54: (A) Ch1, 2hdc, (F) 2hdc, (A) 2hdc, (D) 2hdc, (A) 2hdc, (B) 2hdc, (A) 2hdc, (F) 2hdc, (A) 2hdc, (D) 2hdc, (A) 2hdc, (B) 2hdc, (A) 2hdc, (F) 2hdc, (A) 2hdc, (D) 2hdc, (A) 12hdc, (D) 2hdc, (A) 2hdc, (F) 2hdc, (A) 2hdc, (B) 2hdc, (A) 2hdc, (D) 2hdc, (A) 2hdc, (F) 2hdc, (A) 2hdc, (B) 2hdc, (A) 2hdc, (D) 2hdc, (A) 2hdc, (F) 2hdc, (A) 2hdc, (B) 2hdc, (A) 2hdc, (D) 2hdc, (A) 2hdc, (F) 2hdc, (A) 2hdc.

Rows 55 and 56: (A) Ch1, 2hdc, (F) 2hdc, (A) 2hdc, (D) 2hdc, (A) 2hdc, (B) 2hdc, (A) 2hdc, (F) 2hdc, (A) 2hdc, (D) 2hdc, (A) 2hdc, (B) 2hdc, (A) 2hdc, (F) 2hdc, (A) 2hdc, (D) 2hdc, (A) 2hdc, (B) 8hdc, (A) 2hdc, (D) 2hdc, (A) 2hdc, (F) 2hdc, (A) 2hdc, (B) 2hdc, (A) 2hdc, (D) 2hdc, (A) 2hdc, (F) 2hdc, (A) 2hdc, (B) 2hdc, (A) 2hdc, (D) 2hdc, (A) 2hdc, (F) 2hdc, (A) 2hdc.

Rows 57 and 58: (A) Ch1, 2hdc, (F) 2hdc, (A) 2hdc, (D) 2hdc, (A) 2hdc, (B) 2hdc, (A) 2hdc, (F) 2hdc, (A) 2hdc, (D) 2hdc, (A) 2hdc, (B) 2hdc, (A) 2hdc, (F) 2hdc, (A) 2hdc, (D) 2hdc, (A) 2hdc, (B) 2hdc, (A) 4hdc, (B) 2hdc, (A) 2hdc, (D) 2hdc, (A) 2hdc, (F) 2hdc, (A) 2hdc, (B) 2hdc, (A) 2hdc, (D) 2hdc, (A) 2hdc, (F) 2hdc, (A) 2hdc, (B) 2hdc, (A) 2hdc, (D) 2hdc, (A) 2hdc, (F) 2hdc, (A) 2hdc, (B) 2hdc, (A) 2hdc, (D) 2hdc, (A) 2hdc, (F) 2hdc, (A) 2hdc.

TIP

If you find your yarns are getting rather too tangled, take a breath and try to detangle them before you continue working. Detangling the yarns can be very satisfying, too!

Rows 59 and 60: Repeat Rows 55 and 56.

Rows 61 and 62: Repeat Rows 53 and 54.

Rows 63 and 64: Repeat Rows 51 and 52.

Rows 65 and 66: Repeat Rows 49 and 50.

Rows 67 and 68: Repeat Rows 47 and 48.

Rows 69 and 70: Repeat Rows 45 and 46.

Rows 71 and 72: Repeat Rows 43 and 44.

Rows 73 and 74: Repeat Rows 41 and 42.

Rows 75 and 76: Repeat Rows 39 and 40.

Rows 77 and 78: Repeat Rows 37 and 38.

Rows 79 and 80: Repeat Rows 35 and 36.

Rows 81 and 82: Repeat Rows 33 and 34.

Rows 83 and 84: Repeat Rows 31 and 32.

Rows 85 and 86: Repeat Rows 29 and 30.

Rows 87 and 88: Repeat Rows 27 and 28.

Rows 89 and 90: Repeat Rows 25 and 26.

Rows 91 and 92: Repeat Rows 23 and 24.

Rows 93 and 94: Repeat Rows 21 and 22.

Rows 95 and 96: Repeat Rows 19 and 20.

Rows 97 and 98: Repeat Rows 17 and 18.

Rows 99 and 100: Repeat Rows 15 and 16.

Rows 101 and 102: Repeat Rows 13 and 14.

Rows 103 and 104: Repeat Rows 11 and 12.

Rows 105 and 106: Repeat Rows 9 and 10.

Rows 107 and 108: Repeat Rows 7 and 8.

Rows 109 and 110: Repeat Rows 5 and 6.

Rows 111 and 112: Repeat Rows 3 and 4.

Rows 113 and 114: Repeat Rows 1 and 2.

Don't break yarn.

Row 115 (RS): (A) 100 sl sts across to the end.

Fasten off, and sew in all yarn ends.

Add tassels or pompoms if desired.

WORKING FROM CHART

For each row, work all stitches from 1 to 100. Work Rows 1 to 114 once. Continue with Row 115 of written instructions.

KEY

- ☐ Buttercream Icing
- ▨ Cotton Candy Meringue
- ▨ Orange Cheesecake
- ▨ Pistachio Bundt Cake

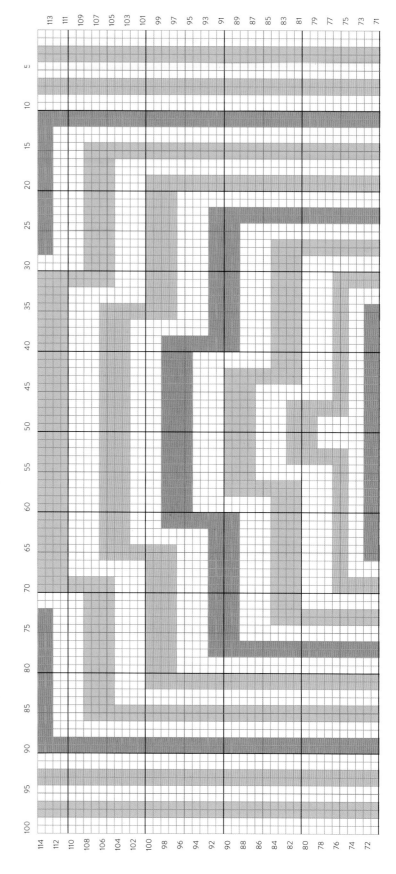

TOP

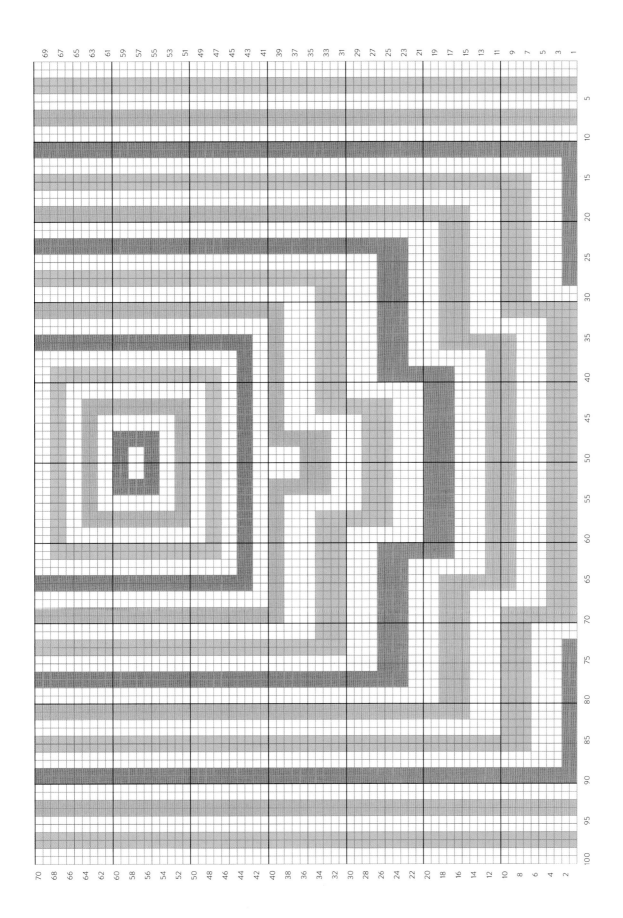

SUNNY
HONEY

The warm tones of the orderly, striped pattern on this design form sunny-coloured rectangular shapes that interlock just like a honeycomb, an effect accentuated by the colours used.

YOU WILL NEED

HOOK

6.5mm (US K/10.5) hook

YARN

Scheepjes Truly Scrumptious (50% recycled polyester (recycled plastic bottles) and 50% acrylic), aran (worsted) weight, 100g (3½oz) = 108m (118yd), in the following shades:

- A: Buttercream Icing (302) x 5 balls
- B: Cotton Candy Meringue (330) x 3 balls
- D: Orange Cheesecake (332) x 2 balls
- E: Custard Pie (341) x 2 balls

YARN BALLS WOUND

- A: 21 x 23g (¾oz)
- B: 10 x 30g (1oz)
- D: 6 x 33g (1⅛oz)
- E: 6 x 33g (1⅛oz)

TENSION (GAUGE)

11 stitches x 9 rows = 10cm (4in) square

FINISHED SIZE

121 x 83cm (47½ x 32½in)

PATTERN

Using a 6.5mm (US K/10.5) hook, chain 95 in Yarn B. Now start in the 2nd chain from the hook.

Rows 1 and 2: (B) Ch1, 2hdc, (A) 2hdc, (D) 2hdc, (A) 2hdc, (E) 2hdc, (A) 2hdc, (B) 2hdc, (A) 2hdc, (B) 2hdc, (A) 2hdc, (E) 2hdc, (A) 2hdc, (D) 2hdc, (A) 2hdc, (B) 2hdc, (A) 2hdc, (D) 2hdc, (A) 2hdc, (E) 2hdc, (A) 2hdc, (B) 2hdc, (A) 10hdc, (B) 2hdc, (A) 2hdc, (E) 2hdc, (A) 2hdc, (D) 2hdc, (A) 2hdc, (B) 2hdc, (A) 2hdc, (D) 2hdc, (A) 2hdc, (E) 2hdc, (A) 2hdc, (B) 2hdc, (A) 2hdc, (B) 2hdc, (A) 2hdc, (E) 2hdc, (A) 2hdc, (D) 2hdc, (A) 2hdc, (B) 2hdc. (94 sts)

Rows 3 and 4: (B) Ch1, 2hdc, (A) 2hdc, (D) 2hdc, (A) 2hdc, (E) 2hdc, (A) 2hdc, (B) 2hdc, (A) 2hdc, (B) 2hdc, (A) 2hdc, (E) 2hdc, (A) 2hdc, (D) 2hdc, (A) 2hdc, (B) 2hdc, (A) 2hdc, (D) 2hdc, (A) 2hdc, (E) 2hdc, (A) 2hdc, (B) 14hdc, (A) 2hdc, (E) 2hdc, (A) 2hdc, (D) 2hdc, (A) 2hdc, (B) 2hdc, (A) 2hdc, (D) 2hdc, (A) 2hdc, (E) 2hdc, (A) 2hdc, (B) 2hdc, (A) 2hdc, (B) 2hdc, (A) 2hdc, (E) 2hdc, (A) 2hdc, (D) 2hdc, (A) 2hdc, (B) 2hdc.

Rows 5 and 6: (B) Ch1, 2hdc, (A) 2hdc, (D) 2hdc, (A) 2hdc, (E) 2hdc, (A) 2hdc, (B) 2hdc, (A) 2hdc, (B) 2hdc, (A) 2hdc, (E) 2hdc, (A) 2hdc, (D) 2hdc, (A) 2hdc, (B) 2hdc, (A) 2hdc, (D) 2hdc, (A) 2hdc, (E) 2hdc, (A) 18hdc, (E) 2hdc, (A) 2hdc, (D) 2hdc, (A) 2hdc, (B) 2hdc, (A) 2hdc, (D) 2hdc, (A) 2hdc, (E) 2hdc, (A) 2hdc, (B) 2hdc, (A) 2hdc, (B) 2hdc, (A) 2hdc, (E) 2hdc, (A) 2hdc, (D) 2hdc, (A) 2hdc, (B) 2hdc.

Rows 7 and 8: (B) Ch1, 2hdc, (A) 2hdc, (D) 2hdc, (A) 2hdc, (E) 2hdc, (A) 2hdc, (B) 2hdc, (A) 2hdc, (B) 2hdc, (A) 2hdc, (E) 2hdc, (A) 2hdc, (D) 2hdc, (A) 2hdc, (B) 2hdc, (A) 2hdc, (D) 2hdc, (A) 2hdc, (E) 22hdc, (A) 2hdc, (D) 2hdc, (A) 2hdc, (B) 2hdc, (A) 2hdc, (D) 2hdc, (A) 2hdc, (E) 2hdc, (A) 2hdc, (B) 2hdc, (A) 2hdc, (B) 2hdc, (A) 2hdc, (E) 2hdc, (A) 2hdc, (D) 2hdc, (A) 2hdc, (B) 2hdc.

Rows 9 and 10: (B) Ch1, 2hdc, (A) 2hdc, (D) 2hdc, (A) 2hdc, (E) 2hdc, (A) 2hdc, (B) 2hdc, (A) 2hdc, (B) 2hdc, (A) 2hdc, (E) 2hdc, (A) 2hdc, (D) 2hdc, (A) 2hdc, (B) 2hdc, (A) 2hdc, (D) 2hdc, (A) 26hdc, (D) 2hdc, (A) 2hdc, (B) 2hdc, (A) 2hdc, (D) 2hdc, (A) 2hdc, (E) 2hdc, (A) 2hdc, (B) 2hdc, (A) 2hdc, (B) 2hdc, (A) 2hdc, (E) 2hdc, (A) 2hdc, (D) 2hdc, (A) 2hdc, (B) 2hdc.

Rows 11 and 12: (B) Ch1, 2hdc, (A) 2hdc, (D) 2hdc, (A) 2hdc, (E) 2hdc, (A) 2hdc, (B) 2hdc, (A) 2hdc, (B) 2hdc, (A) 2hdc, (E) 2hdc, (A) 2hdc, (D) 2hdc, (A) 2hdc, (B) 2hdc, (A) 2hdc, (D) 30hdc, (A) 2hdc, (B) 2hdc, (A) 2hdc, (D) 2hdc, (A) 2hdc, (E) 2hdc, (A) 2hdc, (B) 2hdc, (A) 2hdc, (B) 2hdc, (A) 2hdc, (E) 2hdc, (A) 2hdc, (D) 2hdc, (A) 2hdc, (B) 2hdc.

Rows 13 and 14: (B) Ch1, 2hdc, (A) 2hdc, (D) 2hdc, (A) 2hdc, (E) 2hdc, (A) 2hdc, (B) 2hdc, (A) 2hdc, (B) 2hdc, (A) 2hdc, (E) 2hdc, (A) 2hdc, (D) 2hdc, (A) 2hdc, (B) 2hdc, (A) 34hdc, (B) 2hdc, (A) 2hdc, (D) 2hdc, (A) 2hdc, (E) 2hdc, (A) 2hdc, (B) 2hdc, (A) 2hdc, (B) 2hdc, (A) 2hdc, (E) 2hdc, (A) 2hdc, (D) 2hdc, (A) 2hdc, (B) 2hdc.

Rows 15 and 16: (B) Ch1, 2hdc, (A) 2hdc, (D) 2hdc, (A) 2hdc, (E) 2hdc, (A) 2hdc, (B) 2hdc, (A) 2hdc, (B) 2hdc, (A) 2hdc, (E) 2hdc, (A) 2hdc, (D) 2hdc, (A) 2hdc, (B) 38hdc, (A) 2hdc, (D) 2hdc, (A) 2hdc, (E) 2hdc, (A) 2hdc, (B) 2hdc, (A) 2hdc, (B) 2hdc, (A) 2hdc, (E) 2hdc, (A) 2hdc, (D) 2hdc, (A) 2hdc, (B) 2hdc.

Rows 17 and 18: (B) Ch1, 2hdc, (A) 2hdc, (D) 2hdc, (A) 2hdc, (E) 2hdc, (A) 2hdc, (B) 2hdc, (A) 2hdc, (B) 2hdc, (A) 2hdc, (E) 2hdc, (A) 2hdc, (D) 2hdc, (A) 20hdc, (B) 2hdc, (A) 20hdc, (D) 2hdc, (A) 2hdc, (E) 2hdc, (A) 2hdc, (B) 2hdc, (A) 2hdc, (B) 2hdc, (A) 2hdc, (E) 2hdc, (A) 2hdc, (D) 2hdc, (A) 2hdc, (B) 2hdc.

Rows 19 and 20: (B) Ch1, 2hdc, (A) 2hdc, (D) 2hdc, (A) 2hdc, (E) 2hdc, (A) 2hdc, (B) 2hdc, (A) 2hdc, (B) 2hdc, (A) 2hdc, (E) 2hdc, (A) 2hdc, (D) 20hdc, (A) 2hdc, (B) 2hdc, (A) 2hdc, (D) 20hdc, (A) 2hdc, (E) 2hdc, (A) 2hdc, (B) 2hdc, (A) 2hdc, (B) 2hdc, (A) 2hdc, (E) 2hdc, (A) 2hdc, (D) 2hdc, (A) 2hdc, (B) 2hdc.

Rows 21 and 22: (B) Ch1, 2hdc, (A) 2hdc, (D) 2hdc, (A) 2hdc, (E) 2hdc, (A) 2hdc, (B) 2hdc, (A) 2hdc, (B) 2hdc, (A) 2hdc, (E) 2hdc, (A) 20hdc, (D) 2hdc, (A) 2hdc, (B) 2hdc, (A) 2hdc, (D) 2hdc, (A) 20hdc, (E) 2hdc, (A) 2hdc, (B) 2hdc, (A) 2hdc, (B) 2hdc, (A) 2hdc, (E) 2hdc, (A) 2hdc, (D) 2hdc, (A) 2hdc, (B) 2hdc.

Rows 23 and 24: (B) Ch1, 2hdc, (A) 2hdc, (D) 2hdc, (A) 2hdc, (E) 2hdc, (A) 2hdc, (B) 2hdc, (A) 2hdc, (B) 2hdc, (A) 2hdc, (E) 20hdc, (A) 2hdc, (D) 2hdc, (A) 2hdc, (B) 2hdc, (A) 2hdc, (D) 2hdc, (A) 2hdc, (E) 20hdc, (A) 2hdc, (B) 2hdc, (A) 2hdc, (B) 2hdc, (A) 2hdc, (E) 2hdc, (A) 2hdc, (D) 2hdc, (A) 2hdc, (B) 2hdc.

Rows 25 and 26: (B) Ch1, 2hdc, (A) 2hdc, (D) 2hdc, (A) 2hdc, (E) 2hdc, (A) 2hdc, (B) 2hdc, (A) 2hdc, (B) 2hdc, (A) 20hdc, (E) 2hdc, (A) 2hdc, (D) 2hdc, (A) 2hdc, (B) 2hdc, (A) 2hdc, (D) 2hdc, (A) 2hdc, (E) 2hdc, (A) 20hdc, (B) 2hdc, (A) 2hdc, (B) 2hdc, (A) 2hdc, (E) 2hdc, (A) 2hdc, (D) 2hdc, (A) 2hdc, (B) 2hdc.

Rows 27 and 28: (B) Ch1, 2hdc, (A) 2hdc, (D) 2hdc, (A) 2hdc, (E) 2hdc, (A) 2hdc, (B) 2hdc, (A) 2hdc, (B) 20hdc, (A) 2hdc, (E) 2hdc, (A) 2hdc, (D) 2hdc, (A) 2hdc, (B) 2hdc, (A) 2hdc, (D) 2hdc, (A) 2hdc, (E) 2hdc, (A) 2hdc, (B) 20hdc, (A) 2hdc, (B) 2hdc, (A) 2hdc, (E) 2hdc, (A) 2hdc, (D) 2hdc, (A) 2hdc, (B) 2hdc.

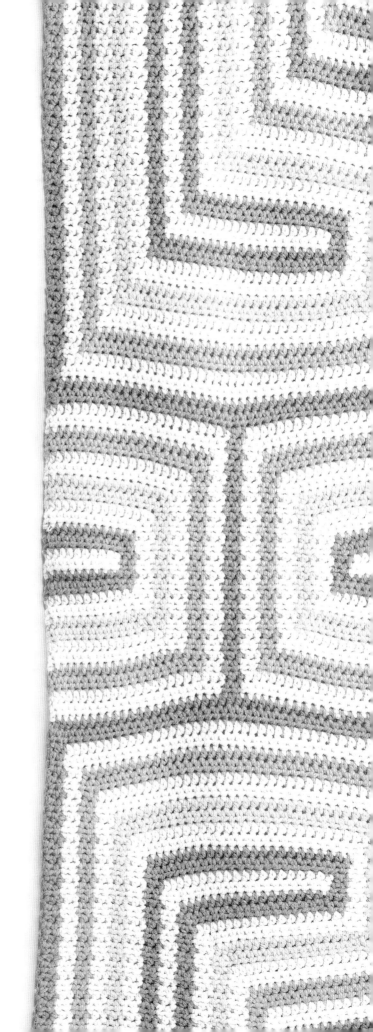

Rows 29 and 30: (B) Ch1, 2hdc, (A) 2hdc, (D) 2hdc, (A) 2hdc, (E) 2hdc, (A) 2hdc, (B) 2hdc, (A) 20hdc, (B) 2hdc, (A) 2hdc, (E) 2hdc, (A) 2hdc, (D) 2hdc, (A) 2hdc, (B) 2hdc, (A) 2hdc, (D) 2hdc, (A) 2hdc, (E) 2hdc, (A) 2hdc, (B) 2hdc, (A) 20hdc, (B) 2hdc, (A) 2hdc, (E) 2hdc, (A) 2hdc, (D) 2hdc, (A) 2hdc, (B) 2hdc.

Rows 31 and 32: (B) Ch1, 2hdc, (A) 2hdc, (D) 2hdc, (A) 2hdc, (E) 2hdc, (A) 2hdc, (B) 24hdc, (A) 2hdc, (E) 2hdc, (A) 2hdc, (D) 2hdc, (A) 2hdc, (B) 2hdc, (A) 2hdc, (D) 2hdc, (A) 2hdc, (E) 2hdc, (A) 2hdc, (B) 24hdc, (A) 2hdc, (E) 2hdc, (A) 2hdc, (D) 2hdc, (A) 2hdc, (B) 2hdc.

Rows 33 and 34: (B) Ch1, 2hdc, (A) 2hdc, (D) 2hdc, (A) 2hdc, (E) 2hdc, (A) 28hdc, (E) 2hdc, (A) 2hdc, (D) 2hdc, (A) 2hdc, (B) 2hdc, (A) 2hdc, (D) 2hdc, (A) 2hdc, (E) 2hdc, (A) 28hdc, (E) 2hdc, (A) 2hdc, (D) 2hdc, (A) 2hdc, (B) 2hdc.

Rows 35 and 36: (B) Ch1, 2hdc, (A) 2hdc, (D) 2hdc, (A) 2hdc, (E) 32hdc, (A) 2hdc, (D) 2hdc, (A) 2hdc, (B) 2hdc, (A) 2hdc, (D) 2hdc, (A) 2hdc, (E) 32hdc, (A) 2hdc, (D) 2hdc, (A) 2hdc, (B) 2hdc.

Rows 37 and 38: (B) Ch1, 2hdc, (A) 2hdc, (D) 2hdc, (A) 36hdc, (D) 2hdc, (A) 2hdc, (B) 2hdc, (A) 2hdc, (D) 2hdc, (A) 36hdc, (D) 2hdc, (A) 2hdc, (B) 2hdc.

Rows 39 and 40: (B) Ch1, 2hdc, (A) 2hdc, (D) 40hdc, (A) 2hdc, (B) 2hdc, (A) 2hdc, (D) 40hdc, (A) 2hdc, (B) 2hdc.

Rows 41 and 42: (B) Ch1, 2hdc, (A) 44hdc, (B) 2hdc, (A) 44hdc, (B) 2hdc.

Rows 43 and 44: (B) Ch1, 94hdc.

Rows 45 and 46: (A) Ch1, 22hdc, (B) 2hdc, (A) 46hdc, (B) 2hdc, (A) 22hdc.

Rows 47 and 48: (D) Ch1, 20hdc, (A) 2hdc, (B) 2hdc, (A) 2hdc, (D) 42hdc, (A) 2hdc, (B) 2hdc, (A) 2hdc, (D) 20hdc.

Rows 49 and 50: (A) Ch1, 18hdc, (D) 2hdc, (A) 2hdc, (B) 2hdc, (A) 2hdc, (D) 2hdc, (A) 38hdc, (D) 2hdc, (A) 2hdc, (B) 2hdc, (A) 2hdc, (D) 2hdc, (A) 18hdc.

Rows 51 and 52: (E) Ch1, 16hdc, (A) 2hdc, (D) 2hdc, (A) 2hdc, (B) 2hdc, (A) 2hdc, (D) 2hdc, (A) 2hdc, (E) 34hdc, (A) 2hdc, (D) 2hdc, (A) 2hdc, (B) 2hdc, (A) 2hdc, (D) 2hdc, (A) 2hdc, (E) 16hdc.

Rows 53 and 54: (A) Ch1, 14hdc, (E) 2hdc, (A) 2hdc, (D) 2hdc, (A) 2hdc, (B) 2hdc, (A) 2hdc, (D) 2hdc, (A) 2hdc, (E) 2hdc, (A) 30hdc, (E) 2hdc, (A) 2hdc, (D) 2hdc, (A) 2hdc, (B) 2hdc, (A) 2hdc, (D) 2hdc, (A) 2hdc, (E) 2hdc, (A) 14hdc.

Rows 55 and 56: (B) Ch1, 12hdc, (A) 2hdc, (E) 2hdc, (A) 2hdc, (D) 2hdc, (A) 2hdc, (B) 2hdc, (A) 2hdc, (D) 2hdc, (A) 2hdc, (E) 2hdc, (A) 2hdc, (B) 26hdc, (A) 2hdc, (E) 2hdc, (A) 2hdc, (D) 2hdc, (A) 2hdc, (B) 2hdc, (A) 2hdc, (D) 2hdc, (A) 2hdc, (E) 2hdc, (A) 2hdc, (B) 12hdc.

Rows 57 and 58: (A) Ch1, 10hdc, (B) 2hdc, (A) 2hdc, (E) 2hdc, (A) 2hdc, (D) 2hdc, (A) 2hdc, (B) 2hdc, (A) 2hdc, (D) 2hdc, (A) 2hdc, (E) 2hdc, (A) 2hdc, (B) 2hdc, (A) 22hdc, (B) 2hdc, (A) 2hdc, (E) 2hdc, (A) 2hdc, (D) 2hdc, (A) 2hdc, (B) 2hdc, (A) 2hdc, (D) 2hdc, (A) 2hdc, (E) 2hdc, (A) 2hdc, (B) 2hdc, (A) 10hdc.

Rows 59 and 60: Repeat Rows 55 and 56.

Rows 61 and 62: Repeat Rows 53 and 54.

Rows 63 and 64: Repeat Rows 51 and 52.

Rows 65 and 66: Repeat Rows 49 and 50.

Rows 67 and 68: Repeat Rows 47 and 48.

Rows 69 and 70: Repeat Rows 45 and 46.

Rows 71 and 72: Repeat Rows 43 and 44.

Rows 73 and 74: Repeat Rows 41 and 42.

Rows 75 and 76: Repeat Rows 39 and 40.

Rows 77 and 78: Repeat Rows 37 and 38.

Rows 79 and 80: Repeat Rows 35 and 36.

Rows 81 and 82: Repeat Rows 33 and 34.

Rows 83 and 84: Repeat Rows 31 and 32.

Rows 85 and 86: Repeat Rows 29 and 30.

Rows 87 and 88: Repeat Rows 27 and 28.

Rows 89 and 90: Repeat Rows 25 and 26.

Rows 91 and 92: Repeat Rows 23 and 24.

Rows 93 and 94: Repeat Rows 21 and 22.

Rows 95 and 96: Repeat Rows 19 and 20.

Rows 97 and 98: Repeat Rows 17 and 18.

Rows 99 and 100: Repeat Rows 15 and 16.

Rows 101 and 102: Repeat Rows 13 and 14.

Rows 103 and 104: Repeat Rows 11 and 12.

Rows 105 and 106: Repeat Rows 9 and 10.

Rows 107 and 108: Repeat Rows 7 and 8.

Rows 109 and 110: Repeat Rows 5 and 6.

Rows 111 and 112: Repeat Rows 3 and 4.

Rows 113 and 114: Repeat Rows 1 and 2.

Don't break yarn.

Row 115 (RS): (B) 94 sl sts across to the end.

Fasten off, and sew in all yarn ends.

Add tassels or pompoms if desired.

TIP

If you are using the chart, you could mark off each square as you go with a pencil, so you can rub it out after. You could also use a little washi tape to mark which line you are working on the chart, if you don't want to use a pencil.

WORKING FROM CHART

For each row, work all stitches from 1 to 94. Work Rows 1 to 114 once. Continue with Row 115 of written instructions.

KEY

☐ Buttercream Icing

▨ Cotton Candy Meringue

▨ Orange Cheesecake

▨ Custard Pie

TOP

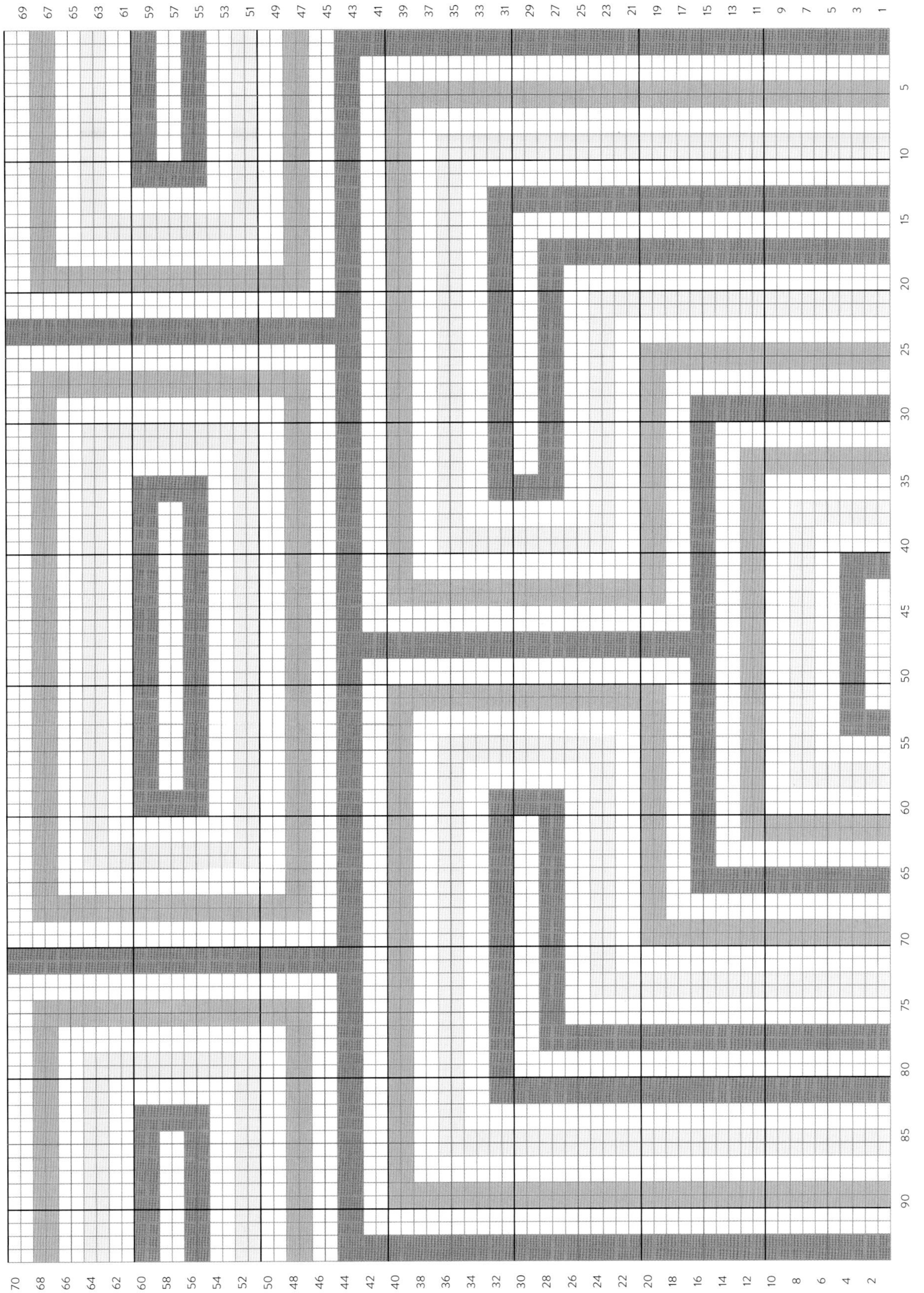

RIBBON
RIVER

Are there three triangular prisms here? Or is this a zigzagging river of horizontal ribbons on a vertically striped background? Or it could be seen as a classic design, based on the geometric Greek key border motif.

YOU WILL NEED

HOOK

6.5mm (US K/10.5) hook

YARN

Scheepjes Truly Scrumptious (50% recycled polyester (recycled plastic bottles) and 50% acrylic), aran (worsted) weight, 100g (3½oz) = 108m (118yd), in the following shades:

- A: Buttercream Icing (302) x 5 balls
- B: Cotton Candy Meringue (330) x 2 balls
- D: Orange Cheesecake (332) x 2 balls
- F: Pistachio Bundt Cake (318) x 2 balls
- K: Sweet Potato Mochi (320) x 2 balls

YARN BALLS WOUND

- A: 13 x 38g (1⅓oz)
- B: 3 x 66g (2⅓oz)
- D: 3 x 66g (2⅓oz)
- F: 3 x 66g (2⅓oz)
- K: 3 x 66g (2⅓oz)

TENSION (GAUGE)

11 stitches x 9 rows = 10cm (4in) square

FINISHED SIZE

120 x 83cm (47¼ x 32½in)

PATTERN

Using a 6.5mm (US K/10.5) hook, chain 93 in Yarn A. Now start in the 2nd chain from the hook.

Row 1 (RS): (A) Ch1, 2hdc, (D) 2hdc, (A) 2hdc, (F) 2hdc, (A) 2hdc, (K) 2hdc, (A) 2hdc, (B) 44hdc, (A) 2hdc, (D) 2hdc, (A) 2hdc, (F) 2hdc, (A) 2hdc, (K) 2hdc, (A) 2hdc, (B) 2hdc, (A) 2hdc, (D) 2hdc, (A) 2hdc, (F) 2hdc, (A) 2hdc, (K) 2hdc, (A) 2hdc, (B) 2hdc, (A) 2hdc. (92 sts)

Row 2 (WS): (A) Ch1, 2hdc, (B) 2hdc, (A) 2hdc, (K) 2hdc, (A) 2hdc, (F) 2hdc, (A) 2hdc, (D) 2hdc, (A) 2hdc, (B) 2hdc, (A) 2hdc, (K) 2hdc, (A) 2hdc, (F) 2hdc, (A) 2hdc, (D) 2hdc, (A) 2hdc, (B) 44hdc, (A) 2hdc, (K) 2hdc, (A) 2hdc, (F) 2hdc, (A) 2hdc, (D) 2hdc, (A) 2hdc. (92 sts)

Row 3 (RS): (A) Ch1, 2hdc, (D) 2hdc, (A) 2hdc, (F) 2hdc, (A) 2hdc, (K) 2hdc, (A) 2hdc, (B) 2hdc, (A) 44hdc, (D) 2hdc, (A) 2hdc, (F) 2hdc, (A) 2hdc, (K) 2hdc, (A) 2hdc, (B) 2hdc, (A) 2hdc, (D) 2hdc, (A) 2hdc, (F) 2hdc, (A) 2hdc, (K) 2hdc, (A) 2hdc, (B) 2hdc, (A) 2hdc.

Row 4 (WS): Ch1, (A) 2hdc, (B) 2hdc, (A) 2hdc, (K) 2hdc, (A) 2hdc, (F) 2hdc, (A) 2hdc, (D) 2hdc, (A) 2hdc, (B) 2hdc, (A) 2hdc, (K) 2hdc, (A) 2hdc, (F) 2hdc, (A) 2hdc, (D) 2hdc, (A) 44hdc, (B) 2hdc, (A) 2hdc, (K) 2hdc, (A) 2hdc, (F) 2hdc, (A) 2hdc, (D) 2hdc, (A) 2hdc.

Row 5 (RS): (A) Ch1, 2hdc, (D) 2hdc, (A) 2hdc, (F) 2hdc, (A) 2hdc, (K) 2hdc, (A) 2hdc, (B) 2hdc, (A) 2hdc, (D) 44hdc, (A) 2hdc, (F) 2hdc, (A) 2hdc, (K) 2hdc, (A) 2hdc, (B) 2hdc, (A) 2hdc, (D) 2hdc, (A) 2hdc, (F) 2hdc, (A) 2hdc, (K) 2hdc, (A) 2hdc, (B) 2hdc, (A) 2hdc.

Row 6 (WS): (A) Ch1, 2hdc, (B) 2hdc, (A) 2hdc, (K) 2hdc, (A) 2hdc, (F) 2hdc, (A) 2hdc, (D) 2hdc, (A) 2hdc, (B) 2hdc, (A) 2hdc, (K) 2hdc, (A) 2hdc, (F) 2hdc, (A) 2hdc, (D) 44hdc, (A) 2hdc, (B) 2hdc, (A) 2hdc, (K) 2hdc, (A) 2hdc, (F) 2hdc, (A) 2hdc, (D) 2hdc, (A) 2hdc.

Row 7 (RS): (A) Ch1, 2hdc, (D) 2hdc, (A) 2hdc, (F) 2hdc, (A) 2hdc, (K) 2hdc, (A) 2hdc, (B) 2hdc, (A) 2hdc, (D) 2hdc, (A) 44hdc, (F) 2hdc, (A) 2hdc, (K) 2hdc, (A) 2hdc, (B) 2hdc, (A) 2hdc, (D) 2hdc, (A) 2hdc, (F) 2hdc, (A) 2hdc, (K) 2hdc, (A) 2hdc, (B) 2hdc, (A) 2hdc.

Row 8 (WS): (A) Ch1, 2hdc, (B) 2hdc, (A) 2hdc, (K) 2hdc, (A) 2hdc, (F) 2hdc, (A) 2hdc, (D) 2hdc, (A) 2hdc, (B) 2hdc, (A) 2hdc, (K) 2hdc, (A) 2hdc, (F) 2hdc, (A) 44hdc, (D) 2hdc, (A) 2hdc, (B) 2hdc, (A) 2hdc, (K) 2hdc, (A) 2hdc, (F) 2hdc, (A) 2hdc, (D) 2hdc, (A) 2hdc.

Row 9 (RS): (A) Ch1, 2hdc, (D) 2hdc, (A) 2hdc, (F) 2hdc, (A) 2hdc, (K) 2hdc, (A) 2hdc, (B) 2hdc, (A) 2hdc, (D) 2hdc, (A) 2hdc, (F) 44hdc, (A) 2hdc, (K) 2hdc, (A) 2hdc, (B) 2hdc, (A) 2hdc, (D) 2hdc, (A) 2hdc, (F) 2hdc, (A) 2hdc, (K) 2hdc, (A) 2hdc, (B) 2hdc, (A) 2hdc.

Row 10 (WS): (A) Ch1, 2hdc, (B) 2hdc, (A) 2hdc, (K) 2hdc, (A) 2hdc, (F) 2hdc, (A) 2hdc, (D) 2hdc, (A) 2hdc, (B) 2hdc, (A) 2hdc, (K) 2hdc, (A) 2hdc, (F) 44hdc, (A) 2hdc, (D) 2hdc, (A) 2hdc, (B) 2hdc, (A) 2hdc, (K) 2hdc, (A) 2hdc, (F) 2hdc, (A) 2hdc, (D) 2hdc, (A) 2hdc.

Row 11 (RS): (A) Ch1, 2hdc, (D) 2hdc, (A) 2hdc, (F) 2hdc, (A) 2hdc, (K) 2hdc, (A) 2hdc, (B) 2hdc, (A) 2hdc, (D) 2hdc, (A) 2hdc, (F) 2hdc, (A) 44hdc, (K) 2hdc, (A) 2hdc, (B) 2hdc, (A) 2hdc, (D) 2hdc, (A) 2hdc, (F) 2hdc, (A) 2hdc, (K) 2hdc, (A) 2hdc, (B) 2hdc, (A) 2hdc.

Row 12 (WS): (A) Ch1, 2hdc, (B) 2hdc, (A) 2hdc, (K) 2hdc, (A) 2hdc, (F) 2hdc, (A) 2hdc, (D) 2hdc, (A) 2hdc, (B) 2hdc, (A) 2hdc, (K) 2hdc, (A) 44hdc, (F) 2hdc, (A) 2hdc, (D) 2hdc, (A) 2hdc, (B) 2hdc, (A) 2hdc, (K) 2hdc, (A) 2hdc, (F) 2hdc, (A) 2hdc, (D) 2hdc, (A) 2hdc.

Row 13 (RS): (A) Ch1, 2hdc, (D) 2hdc, (A) 2hdc, (F) 2hdc, (A) 2hdc, (K) 2hdc, (A) 2hdc, (B) 2hdc, (A) 2hdc, (D) 2hdc, (A) 2hdc, (F) 2hdc, (A) 2hdc, (K) 44hdc, (A) 2hdc, (B) 2hdc, (A) 2hdc, (D) 2hdc, (A) 2hdc, (F) 2hdc, (A) 2hdc, (K) 2hdc, (A) 2hdc, (B) 2hdc, (A) 2hdc.

Row 14 (WS): (A) Ch1, 2hdc, (B) 2hdc, (A) 2hdc, (K) 2hdc, (A) 2hdc, (F) 2hdc, (A) 2hdc, (D) 2hdc, (A) 2hdc, (B) 2hdc, (A) 2hdc, (K) 44hdc, (A) 2hdc, (F) 2hdc, (A) 2hdc, (D) 2hdc, (A) 2hdc, (B) 2hdc, (A) 2hdc, (K) 2hdc, (A) 2hdc, (F) 2hdc, (A) 2hdc, (D) 2hdc, (A) 2hdc.

Row 15 (RS): (A) Ch1, 2hdc, (D) 2hdc, (A) 2hdc, (F) 2hdc, (A) 2hdc, (K) 2hdc, (A) 2hdc, (B) 2hdc, (A) 2hdc, (D) 2hdc, (A) 2hdc, (F) 2hdc, (A) 2hdc, (K) 2hdc, (A) 44hdc, (B) 2hdc, (A) 2hdc, (D) 2hdc, (A) 2hdc, (F) 2hdc, (A) 2hdc, (K) 2hdc, (A) 2hdc, (B) 2hdc, (A) 2hdc.

Row 16 (WS): (A) Ch1, 2hdc, (B) 2hdc, (A) 2hdc, (K) 2hdc, (A) 2hdc, (F) 2hdc, (A) 2hdc, (D) 2hdc, (A) 2hdc, (B) 2hdc, (A) 44hdc, (K) 2hdc, (A) 2hdc, (F) 2hdc, (A) 2hdc, (D) 2hdc, (A) 2hdc, (B) 2hdc, (A) 2hdc, (K) 2hdc, (A) 2hdc, (F) 2hdc, (A) 2hdc, (D) 2hdc, (A) 2hdc.

Row 17 (RS): (A) Ch1, 2hdc, (D) 2hdc, (A) 2hdc, (F) 2hdc, (A) 2hdc, (K) 2hdc, (A) 2hdc, (B) 2hdc, (A) 2hdc, (D) 2hdc, (A) 2hdc, (F) 2hdc, (A) 2hdc, (K) 2hdc, (A) 2hdc, (B) 44hdc, (A) 2hdc, (D) 2hdc, (A) 2hdc, (F) 2hdc, (A) 2hdc, (K) 2hdc, (A) 2hdc, (B) 2hdc, (A) 2hdc.

Row 18 (WS): (A) Ch1, 2hdc, (B) 2hdc, (A) 2hdc, (K) 2hdc, (A) 2hdc, (F) 2hdc, (A) 2hdc, (D) 2hdc, (A) 2hdc, (B) 44hdc, (A) 2hdc, (K) 2hdc, (A) 2hdc, (F) 2hdc, (A) 2hdc, (D) 2hdc, (A) 2hdc, (B) 2hdc, (A) 2hdc, (K) 2hdc, (A) 2hdc, (F) 2hdc, (A) 2hdc, (D) 2hdc, (A) 2hdc.

Row 19 (RS): (A) Ch1, 2hdc, (D) 2hdc, (A) 2hdc, (F) 2hdc, (A) 2hdc, (K) 2hdc, (A) 2hdc, (B) 2hdc, (A) 2hdc, (D) 2hdc, (A) 2hdc, (F) 2hdc, (A) 2hdc, (K) 2hdc, (A) 2hdc, (B) 2hdc, (A) 44hdc, (D) 2hdc, (A) 2hdc, (F) 2hdc, (A) 2hdc, (K) 2hdc, (A) 2hdc, (B) 2hdc, (A) 2hdc.

Row 20 (WS): (A) Ch1, 2hdc, (B) 2hdc, (A) 2hdc, (K) 2hdc, (A) 2hdc, (F) 2hdc, (A) 2hdc, (D) 2hdc, (A) 44hdc, (B) 2hdc, (A) 2hdc, (K) 2hdc, (A) 2hdc, (F) 2hdc, (A) 2hdc, (D) 2hdc, (A) 2hdc, (B) 2hdc, (A) 2hdc, (K) 2hdc, (A) 2hdc, (F) 2hdc, (A) 2hdc, (D) 2hdc, (A) 2hdc.

Row 21 (RS): (A) Ch1, 2hdc, (D) 2hdc, (A) 2hdc, (F) 2hdc, (A) 2hdc, (K) 2hdc, (A) 2hdc, (B) 2hdc, (A) 2hdc, (D) 2hdc, (A) 2hdc, (F) 2hdc, (A) 2hdc, (K) 2hdc, (A) 2hdc, (B) 2hdc, (A) 2hdc, (D) 44hdc, (A) 2hdc, (F) 2hdc, (A) 2hdc, (K) 2hdc, (A) 2hdc, (B) 2hdc, (A) 2hdc.

Row 22 (WS): (A) Ch1, 2hdc, (B) 2hdc, (A) 2hdc, (K) 2hdc, (A) 2hdc, (F) 2hdc, (A) 2hdc, (D) 44hdc, (A) 2hdc, (B) 2hdc, (A) 2hdc, (K) 2hdc, (A) 2hdc, (F) 2hdc, (A) 2hdc, (D) 2hdc, (A) 2hdc, (B) 2hdc, (A) 2hdc, (K) 2hdc, (A) 2hdc, (F) 2hdc, (A) 2hdc, (D) 2hdc, (A) 2hdc.

Row 23 (RS): (A) Ch1, 2hdc, (D) 2hdc, (A) 2hdc, (F) 2hdc, (A) 2hdc, (K) 2hdc, (A) 2hdc, (B) 2hdc, (A) 2hdc, (D) 2hdc, (A) 2hdc, (F) 2hdc, (A) 2hdc, (K) 2hdc, (A) 2hdc, (B) 2hdc, (A) 2hdc, (D) 2hdc, (A) 44hdc, (F) 2hdc, (A) 2hdc, (K) 2hdc, (A) 2hdc, (B) 2hdc, (A) 2hdc.

Row 24 (WS): (A) Ch1, 2hdc, (B) 2hdc, (A) 2hdc, (K) 2hdc, (A) 2hdc, (F) 2hdc, (A) 44hdc, (D) 2hdc, (A) 2hdc, (B) 2hdc, (A) 2hdc, (K) 2hdc, (A) 2hdc, (F) 2hdc, (A) 2hdc, (D) 2hdc, (A) 2hdc, (B) 2hdc, (A) 2hdc, (K) 2hdc, (A) 2hdc, (F) 2hdc, (A) 2hdc, (D) 2hdc, (A) 2hdc.

Row 25 (RS): (A) Ch1, 2hdc, (D) 2hdc, (A) 2hdc, (F) 2hdc, (A) 2hdc, (K) 2hdc, (A) 2hdc, (B) 2hdc, (A) 2hdc, (D) 2hdc, (A) 2hdc, (F) 2hdc, (A) 2hdc, (K) 2hdc, (A) 2hdc, (B) 2hdc, (A) 2hdc, (D) 2hdc, (A) 2hdc, (F) 44hdc, (A) 2hdc, (K) 2hdc, (A) 2hdc, (B) 2hdc, (A) 2hdc.

Row 26 (WS): (A) Ch1, 2hdc, (B) 2hdc, (A) 2hdc, (K) 2hdc, (A) 2hdc, (F) 44hdc, (A) 2hdc, (D) 2hdc, (A) 2hdc, (B) 2hdc, (A) 2hdc, (K) 2hdc, (A) 2hdc, (F) 2hdc, (A) 2hdc, (D) 2hdc, (A) 2hdc, (B) 2hdc, (A) 2hdc, (K) 2hdc, (A) 2hdc, (F) 2hdc, (A) 2hdc, (D) 2hdc, (A) 2hdc.

Rows 27 and 28: Repeat Rows 23 and 24.

Rows 29 and 30: Repeat Rows 21 and 22.

Rows 31 and 32: Repeat Rows 19 and 20.

Rows 33 and 34: Repeat Rows 17 and 18.

Rows 35 and 36: Repeat Rows 15 and 16.

Rows 37 and 38: Repeat Rows 13 and 14.

Rows 39 and 40: Repeat Rows 11 and 12.

Rows 41 and 42: Repeat Rows 9 and 10.

Rows 43 and 44: Repeat Rows 7 and 8.

Rows 45 and 46: Repeat Rows 5 and 6.

Rows 47 and 48: Repeat Rows 3 and 4.

Rows 49 and 50: Repeat Rows 1 and 2.

Row 51 (RS): (A) Ch1, 2hdc, (D) 2hdc, (A) 2hdc, (F) 2hdc, (A) 2hdc, (K) 2hdc, (A) 44hdc, (B) 2hdc, (A) 2hdc, (D) 2hdc, (A) 2hdc, (F) 2hdc, (A) 2hdc, (K) 2hdc, (A) 2hdc, (B) 2hdc, (A) 2hdc, (D) 2hdc, (A) 2hdc, (F) 2hdc, (A) 2hdc, (K) 2hdc, (A) 2hdc, (B) 2hdc, (A) 2hdc.

Row 52 (WS): (A) Ch1, 2hdc, (B) 2hdc, (A) 2hdc, (K) 2hdc, (A) 2hdc, (F) 2hdc, (A) 2hdc, (D) 2hdc, (A) 2hdc, (B) 2hdc, (A) 2hdc, (K) 2hdc, (A) 2hdc, (F) 2hdc, (A) 2hdc, (D) 2hdc, (A) 2hdc, (B) 2hdc, (A) 44hdc, (K) 2hdc, (A) 2hdc, (F) 2hdc, (A) 2hdc, (D) 2hdc, (A) 2hdc.

Row 53 (RS): (A) Ch1, 2hdc, (D) 2hdc, (A) 2hdc, (F) 2hdc, (A) 2hdc, (K) 44hdc, (A) 2hdc, (B) 2hdc, (A) 2hdc, (D) 2hdc, (A) 2hdc, (F) 2hdc, (A) 2hdc, (K) 2hdc, (A) 2hdc, (B) 2hdc, (A) 2hdc, (D) 2hdc, (A) 2hdc, (F) 2hdc, (A) 2hdc, (K) 2hdc, (A) 2hdc, (B) 2hdc, (A) 2hdc.

Row 54 (WS): (A) Ch1, 2hdc, (B) 2hdc, (A) 2hdc, (K) 2hdc, (A) 2hdc, (F) 2hdc, (A) 2hdc, (D) 2hdc, (A) 2hdc, (B) 2hdc, (A) 2hdc, (K) 2hdc, (A) 2hdc, (F) 2hdc, (A) 2hdc, (D) 2hdc, (A) 2hdc, (B) 2hdc, (A) 2hdc, (K) 44hdc, (A) 2hdc, (F) 2hdc, (A) 2hdc, (D) 2hdc, (A) 2hdc.

Row 55 (RS): (A) Ch1, 2hdc, (D) 2hdc, (A) 2hdc, (F) 2hdc, (A) 44hdc, (K) 2hdc, (A) 2hdc, (B) 2hdc, (A) 2hdc, (D) 2hdc, (A) 2hdc, (F) 2hdc, (A) 2hdc, (K) 2hdc, (A) 2hdc, (B) 2hdc, (A) 2hdc, (D) 2hdc, (A) 2hdc, (F) 2hdc, (A) 2hdc, (K) 2hdc, (A) 2hdc, (B) 2hdc, (A) 2hdc.

Row 56 (WS): (A) Ch1, 2hdc, (B) 2hdc, (A) 2hdc, (K) 2hdc, (A) 2hdc, (F) 2hdc, (A) 2hdc, (D) 2hdc, (A) 2hdc, (B) 2hdc, (A) 2hdc, (K) 2hdc, (A) 2hdc, (F) 2hdc, (A) 2hdc, (D) 2hdc, (A) 2hdc, (B) 2hdc, (A) 2hdc, (K) 2hdc, (A) 44hdc, (F) 2hdc, (A) 2hdc, (D) 2hdc, (A) 2hdc.

Row 57 (RS): (A) Ch1, 2hdc, (D) 2hdc, (A) 2hdc, (F) 44hdc, (A) 2hdc, (K) 2hdc, (A) 2hdc, (B) 2hdc, (A) 2hdc, (D) 2hdc, (A) 2hdc, (F) 2hdc, (A) 2hdc, (K) 2hdc, (A) 2hdc, (B) 2hdc, (A) 2hdc, (D) 2hdc, (A) 2hdc, (F) 2hdc, (A) 2hdc, (K) 2hdc, (A) 2hdc, (B) 2hdc, (A) 2hdc.

Row 58 (WS): (A) Ch1, 2hdc, (B) 2hdc, (A) 2hdc, (K) 2hdc, (A) 2hdc, (F) 2hdc, (A) 2hdc, (D) 2hdc, (A) 2hdc, (B) 2hdc, (A) 2hdc, (K) 2hdc, (A) 2hdc, (F) 2hdc, (A) 2hdc, (D) 2hdc, (A) 2hdc, (B) 2hdc, (A) 2hdc, (K) 2hdc, (A) 2hdc, (F) 44hdc, (A) 2hdc, (D) 2hdc, (A) 2hdc.

Rows 59 and 60: Repeat Rows 55 and 56.

Rows 61 and 62: Repeat Rows 53 and 54.

Rows 63 and 64: Repeat Rows 51 and 52.

Rows 65 to 114: Repeat Rows 1 to 50.

Don't break yarn.

Row 115 (RS): (A) 92 sl sts across to the end.

Fasten off, and sew in all yarn ends.

Add tassels or pompoms if desired.

TIP

The starting chain for each blanket design is usually the same colour as the first stitch of the first row on the chart. But be sure to check this before you start your blanket.

WORKING FROM CHART

For each row, work all stitches from 1 to 92. Work Rows 1 to 64 once, then repeat Rows 1 to 50 once more. Continue with Row 115 of written instructions.

KEY

Buttercream Icing

Cotton Candy Meringue

Orange Cheesecake

Pistachio Bundt Cake

Sweet Potato Mochi

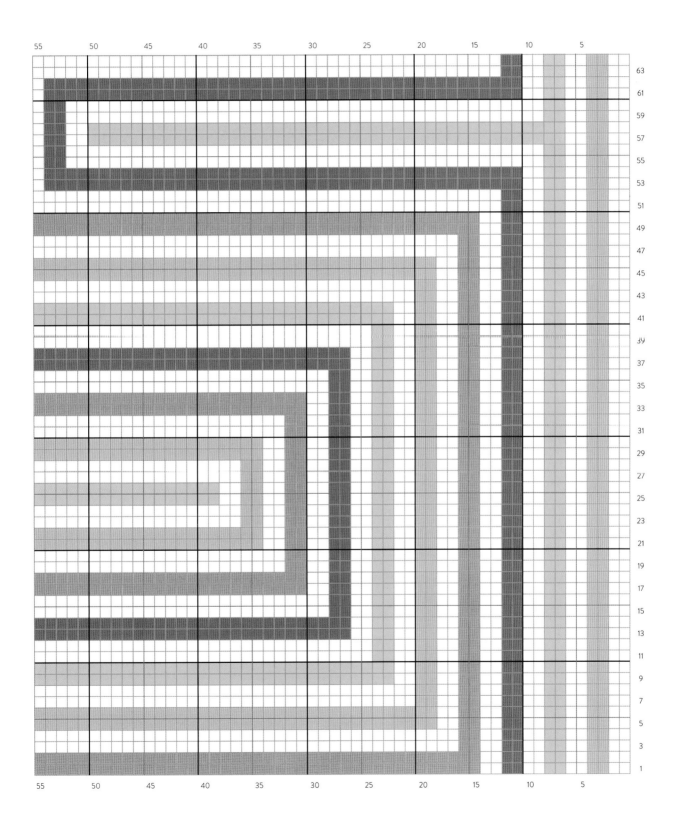

COOL
CONTOURS

The cool-coloured lines on this design resemble contour lines on a map, because they all follow the same path – but in this case they cleverly reveal the outline of a diamond shape.

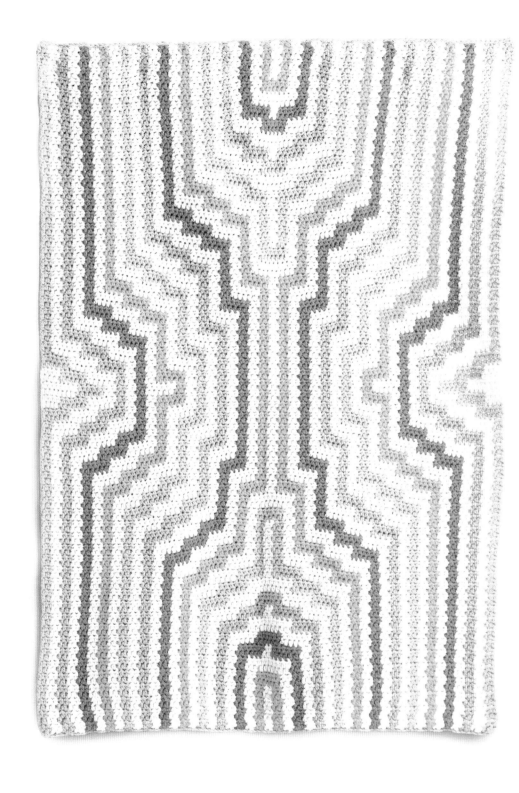

YOU WILL NEED

HOOK

6.5mm (US K/10.5) hook

YARN

Scheepjes Truly Scrumptious (50% recycled polyester (recycled plastic bottles) and 50% acrylic), aran (worsted) weight, 100g (3½oz) = 108m (118yd), in the following shades:

- A: Buttercream Icing (302) x 5 balls
- G: Mint Whoopie Pie (340) x 2 balls
- H: Bubblegum Ice Cream (355) x 2 balls
- I: French Blue Macaron (343) x 2 balls
- J: Lavender Slice (334) x 2 balls

YARN BALLS WOUND

- A: 23 x 21g (¾oz)
- G: 6 x 33g (1⅛oz)
- H: 6 x 33g (1⅛oz)
- I: 6 x 33g (1⅛oz)
- J: 6 x 33g (1⅛oz)

TENSION (GAUGE)

11 stitches x 9 rows = 10cm (4in) square

FINISHED SIZE

115 x 83cm (45in x 32½in)

PATTERN

Using a 6.5mm (US K/10.5) hook, chain 95 in Yarn I. Now start in the 2nd chain from the hook.

Rows 1 to 9: (I) Ch1, 2hdc, (A) 2hdc, (J) 2hdc, (A) 2hdc, (H) 2hdc, (A) 2hdc, (G) 2hdc, (A) 2hdc, (I) 2hdc, (A) 2hdc, (J) 2hdc, (A) 2hdc, (H) 2hdc, (A) 2hdc, (G) 2hdc, (A) 2hdc, (I) 2hdc, (A) 2hdc, (J) 2hdc, (A) 2hdc, (H) 2hdc, (A) 2hdc, (G) 2hdc, (A) 2hdc, (G) 2hdc, (A) 2hdc, (H) 2hdc, (A) 2hdc, (J) 2hdc, (A) 2hdc, (I) 2hdc, (A) 2hdc, (G) 2hdc, (A) 2hdc, (H) 2hdc, (A) 2hdc, (J) 2hdc, (A) 2hdc, (I) 2hdc, (A) 2hdc, (G) 2hdc, (A) 2hdc, (H) 2hdc, (A) 2hdc, (J) 2hdc, (A) 2hdc, (I) 2hdc. (94 sts)

Rows 10 and 11: (I) Ch1, 2hdc, (A) 2hdc, (J) 2hdc, (A) 2hdc, (H) 2hdc, (A) 2hdc, (G) 2hdc, (A) 2hdc, (I) 2hdc, (A) 2hdc, (J) 2hdc, (A) 2hdc, (H) 2hdc, (A) 2hdc, (G) 2hdc, (A) 2hdc, (I) 2hdc, (A) 2hdc, (J) 2hdc, (A) 2hdc, (H) 2hdc, (A) 2hdc, (G) 6hdc, (A) 2hdc, (H) 2hdc, (A) 2hdc, (J) 2hdc, (A) 2hdc, (I) 2hdc, (A) 2hdc, (G) 2hdc, (A) 2hdc, (H) 2hdc, (A) 2hdc, (J) 2hdc, (A) 2hdc, (I) 2hdc, (A) 2hdc, (G) 2hdc, (A) 2hdc, (H) 2hdc, (A) 2hdc, (J) 2hdc, (A) 2hdc, (I) 2hdc.

Rows 12 and 13: (I) Ch1, 2hdc, (A) 2hdc, (J) 2hdc, (A) 2hdc, (H) 2hdc, (A) 2hdc, (G) 2hdc, (A) 2hdc, (I) 2hdc, (A) 2hdc, (J) 2hdc, (A) 2hdc, (H) 2hdc, (A) 2hdc, (G) 2hdc, (A) 2hdc, (I) 2hdc, (A) 2hdc, (J) 2hdc, (A) 2hdc, (H) 2hdc, (A) 10hdc, (H) 2hdc, (A) 2hdc, (J) 2hdc, (A) 2hdc, (I) 2hdc, (A) 2hdc, (G) 2hdc, (A) 2hdc, (H) 2hdc, (A) 2hdc, (J) 2hdc, (A) 2hdc, (I) 2hdc, (A) 2hdc, (G) 2hdc, (A) 2hdc, (H) 2hdc, (A) 2hdc, (J) 2hdc, (A) 2hdc, (I) 2hdc.

Rows 14 and 15: (I) Ch1, 2hdc, (A) 2hdc, (J) 2hdc, (A) 2hdc, (H) 2hdc, (A) 2hdc, (G) 2hdc, (A) 2hdc, (I) 2hdc, (A) 2hdc, (J) 2hdc, (A) 2hdc, (H) 2hdc, (A) 2hdc, (G) 2hdc, (A) 2hdc, (I) 2hdc, (A) 2hdc, (J) 2hdc, (A) 2hdc, (H) 6hdc, (A) 2hdc, (H) 6hdc, (A) 2hdc, (J) 2hdc, (A) 2hdc, (I) 2hdc, (A) 2hdc, (G) 2hdc, (A) 2hdc, (H) 2hdc, (A) 2hdc, (J) 2hdc, (A) 2hdc, (I) 2hdc, (A) 2hdc, (G) 2hdc, (A) 2hdc, (H) 2hdc, (A) 2hdc, (J) 2hdc, (A) 2hdc, (I) 2hdc.

Rows 16 and 17: (I) Ch1, 2hdc, (A) 2hdc, (J) 2hdc, (A) 2hdc, (H) 2hdc, (A) 2hdc, (G) 2hdc, (A) 2hdc, (I) 2hdc, (A) 2hdc, (J) 2hdc, (A) 2hdc, (H) 2hdc, (A) 2hdc, (G) 2hdc, (A) 2hdc, (I) 2hdc, (A) 2hdc, (J) 2hdc, (A) 6hdc, (H) 6hdc, (A) 6hdc, (J) 2hdc, (A) 2hdc, (I) 2hdc, (A) 2hdc, (G) 2hdc, (A) 2hdc, (H) 2hdc, (A) 2hdc, (J) 2hdc, (A) 2hdc, (I) 2hdc, (A) 2hdc, (G) 2hdc, (A) 2hdc, (H) 2hdc, (A) 2hdc, (J) 2hdc, (A) 2hdc, (I) 2hdc.

Rows 18 and 19: (I) Ch1, 2hdc, (A) 2hdc, (J) 2hdc, (A) 2hdc, (H) 2hdc, (A) 2hdc, (G) 2hdc, (A) 2hdc, (I) 2hdc, (A) 2hdc, (J) 2hdc, (A) 2hdc, (H) 2hdc, (A) 2hdc, (G) 2hdc, (A) 2hdc, (I) 2hdc, (A) 2hdc, (J) 6hdc, (A) 10hdc, (J) 6hdc, (A) 2hdc, (I) 2hdc, (A) 2hdc, (G) 2hdc, (A) 2hdc, (H) 2hdc, (A) 2hdc, (J) 2hdc, (A) 2hdc, (I) 2hdc, (A) 2hdc, (G) 2hdc, (A) 2hdc, (H) 2hdc, (A) 2hdc, (J) 2hdc, (A) 2hdc, (I) 2hdc.

Rows 20 and 21: (I) Ch1, 2hdc, (A) 2hdc, (J) 2hdc, (A) 2hdc, (H) 2hdc, (A) 2hdc, (G) 2hdc, (A) 2hdc, (I) 2hdc, (A) 2hdc, (J) 2hdc, (A) 2hdc, (H) 2hdc, (A) 2hdc, (G) 2hdc, (A) 2hdc, (I) 2hdc, (A) 6hdc, (J) 6hdc, (A) 2hdc, (J) 6hdc, (A) 6hdc, (I) 2hdc, (A) 2hdc, (G) 2hdc, (A) 2hdc, (H) 2hdc, (A) 2hdc, (J) 2hdc, (A) 2hdc, (I) 2hdc, (A) 2hdc, (G) 2hdc, (A) 2hdc, (H) 2hdc, (A) 2hdc, (J) 2hdc, (A) 2hdc, (I) 2hdc.

Rows 22 and 23: (I) Ch1, 2hdc, (A) 2hdc, (J) 2hdc, (A) 2hdc, (H) 2hdc, (A) 2hdc, (G) 2hdc, (A) 2hdc, (I) 2hdc, (A) 2hdc, (J) 2hdc, (A) 2hdc, (H) 2hdc, (A) 2hdc, (G) 2hdc, (A) 2hdc, (I) 6hdc, (A) 6hdc, (J) 6hdc, (A) 6hdc, (I) 6hdc, (A) 2hdc, (G) 2hdc, (A) 2hdc, (H) 2hdc, (A) 2hdc, (J) 2hdc, (A) 2hdc, (I) 2hdc, (A) 2hdc, (G) 2hdc, (A) 2hdc, (H) 2hdc, (A) 2hdc, (J) 2hdc, (A) 2hdc, (I) 2hdc.

Rows 24 and 25: (I) Ch1, 2hdc, (A) 2hdc, (J) 2hdc, (A) 2hdc, (H) 2hdc, (A) 2hdc, (G) 2hdc, (A) 2hdc, (I) 2hdc, (A) 2hdc, (J) 2hdc, (A) 2hdc, (H) 2hdc, (A) 2hdc, (G) 2hdc, (A) 6hdc, (I) 6hdc, (A) 10hdc, (I) 6hdc, (A) 6hdc, (G) 2hdc, (A) 2hdc, (H) 2hdc, (A) 2hdc, (J) 2hdc, (A) 2hdc, (I) 2hdc, (A) 2hdc, (G) 2hdc, (A) 2hdc, (H) 2hdc, (A) 2hdc, (J) 2hdc, (A) 2hdc, (I) 2hdc.

Rows 26 and 27: (I) Ch1, 2hdc, (A) 2hdc, (J) 2hdc, (A) 2hdc, (H) 2hdc, (A) 2hdc, (G) 2hdc, (A) 2hdc, (I) 2hdc, (A) 2hdc, (J) 2hdc, (A) 2hdc, (H) 2hdc, (A) 2hdc, (G) 6hdc, (A) 6hdc, (I) 6hdc, (A) 2hdc, (I) 6hdc, (A) 6hdc, (G) 6hdc, (A) 2hdc, (H) 2hdc, (A) 2hdc, (J) 2hdc, (A) 2hdc, (I) 2hdc, (A) 2hdc, (G) 2hdc, (A) 2hdc, (H) 2hdc, (A) 2hdc, (J) 2hdc, (A) 2hdc, (I) 2hdc.

Rows 28 and 29: (I) Ch1, 2hdc, (A) 2hdc, (J) 2hdc, (A) 2hdc, (H) 2hdc, (A) 2hdc, (G) 2hdc, (A) 2hdc, (I) 2hdc, (A) 2hdc, (J) 2hdc, (A) 2hdc, (H) 2hdc, (A) 6hdc, (G) 6hdc, (A) 6hdc, (I) 2hdc, (A) 2hdc, (I) 2hdc, (A) 6hdc, (G) 6hdc, (A) 6hdc, (H) 2hdc, (A) 2hdc, (J) 2hdc, (A) 2hdc, (I) 2hdc, (A) 2hdc, (G) 2hdc, (A) 2hdc, (H) 2hdc, (A) 2hdc, (J) 2hdc, (A) 2hdc, (I) 2hdc.

Rows 30 and 31: (I) Ch1, 2hdc, (A) 2hdc, (J) 2hdc, (A) 2hdc, (H) 2hdc, (A) 2hdc, (G) 2hdc, (A) 2hdc, (I) 2hdc, (A) 2hdc, (J) 2hdc, (A) 2hdc, (H) 6hdc, (A) 6hdc, (G) 6hdc, (A) 2hdc, (I) 2hdc, (A) 2hdc, (I) 2hdc, (A) 2hdc, (G) 6hdc, (A) 6hdc, (H) 6hdc, (A) 2hdc, (J) 2hdc, (A) 2hdc, (I) 2hdc, (A) 2hdc, (G) 2hdc, (A) 2hdc, (H) 2hdc, (A) 2hdc, (J) 2hdc, (A) 2hdc, (I) 2hdc.

Rows 32 and 33: (I) Ch1, 2hdc, (A) 2hdc, (J) 2hdc, (A) 2hdc, (H) 2hdc, (A) 2hdc, (G) 2hdc, (A) 2hdc, (I) 2hdc, (A) 2hdc, (J) 2hdc, (A) 6hdc, (H) 6hdc, (A) 6hdc, (G) 2hdc, (A) 2hdc, (I) 2hdc, (A) 2hdc, (I) 2hdc, (A) 2hdc, (G) 2hdc, (A) 6hdc, (H) 6hdc, (A) 6hdc, (J) 2hdc, (A) 2hdc, (I) 2hdc, (A) 2hdc, (G) 2hdc, (A) 2hdc, (H) 2hdc, (A) 2hdc, (J) 2hdc, (A) 2hdc, (I) 2hdc.

Rows 34 and 35: (I) Ch1, 2hdc, (A) 2hdc, (J) 2hdc, (A) 2hdc, (H) 2hdc, (A) 2hdc, (G) 2hdc, (A) 2hdc, (I) 2hdc, (A) 2hdc, (J) 6hdc, (A) 6hdc, (H) 6hdc, (A) 2hdc, (G) 2hdc, (A) 2hdc, (I) 2hdc, (A) 2hdc, (G) 2hdc, (A) 2hdc, (H) 6hdc, (A) 6hdc, (J) 6hdc, (A) 2hdc, (I) 2hdc, (A) 2hdc, (G) 2hdc, (A) 2hdc, (H) 2hdc, (A) 2hdc, (J) 2hdc, (A) 2hdc, (I) 2hdc.

Rows 36 and 37: (I) Ch1, 2hdc, (A) 2hdc, (J) 2hdc, (A) 2hdc, (H) 2hdc, (A) 2hdc, (G) 2hdc, (A) 2hdc, (I) 2hdc, (A) 6hdc, (J) 6hdc, (A) 6hdc, (H) 2hdc, (A) 2hdc, (G) 2hdc, (A) 2hdc, (I) 6hdc, (A) 2hdc, (G) 2hdc, (A) 2hdc, (H) 2hdc, (A) 6hdc, (J) 6hdc, (A) 6hdc, (I) 2hdc, (A) 2hdc, (G) 2hdc, (A) 2hdc, (H) 2hdc, (A) 2hdc, (J) 2hdc, (A) 2hdc, (I) 2hdc.

Rows 38 and 39: (I) Ch1, 2hdc, (A) 2hdc, (J) 2hdc, (A) 2hdc, (H) 2hdc, (A) 2hdc, (G) 2hdc, (A) 2hdc, (I) 6hdc, (A) 6hdc, (J) 6hdc, (A) 2hdc, (H) 2hdc, (A) 2hdc, (G) 2hdc, (A) 10hdc, (G) 2hdc, (A) 2hdc, (H) 2hdc, (A) 2hdc, (J) 6hdc, (A) 6hdc, (I) 6hdc, (A) 2hdc, (G) 2hdc, (A) 2hdc, (H) 2hdc, (A) 2hdc, (J) 2hdc, (A) 2hdc, (I) 2hdc.

Rows 40 and 41: (I) Ch1, 2hdc, (A) 2hdc, (J) 2hdc, (A) 2hdc, (H) 2hdc, (A) 2hdc, (G) 2hdc, (A) 6hdc, (I) 6hdc, (A) 6hdc, (J) 2hdc, (A) 2hdc, (H) 2hdc, (A) 2hdc, (G) 6hdc, (A) 2hdc, (G) 6hdc, (A) 2hdc, (H) 2hdc, (A) 2hdc, (J) 2hdc, (A) 6hdc, (I) 6hdc, (A) 6hdc, (G) 2hdc, (A) 2hdc, (H) 2hdc, (A) 2hdc, (J) 2hdc, (A) 2hdc, (I) 2hdc.

Rows 42 and 43: (I) Ch1, 2hdc, (A) 2hdc, (J) 2hdc, (A) 2hdc, (H) 2hdc, (A) 2hdc, (G) 6hdc, (A) 6hdc, (I) 6hdc, (A) 2hdc, (J) 2hdc, (A) 2hdc, (H) 2hdc, (A) 6hdc, (G) 2hdc, (A) 2hdc, (G) 2hdc, (A) 6hdc, (H) 2hdc, (A) 2hdc, (J) 2hdc, (A) 2hdc, (I) 6hdc, (A) 6hdc, (G) 6hdc, (A) 2hdc, (H) 2hdc, (A) 2hdc, (J) 2hdc, (A) 2hdc, (I) 2hdc.

Rows 44 and 45: (I) Ch1, 2hdc, (A) 2hdc, (J) 2hdc, (A) 2hdc, (H) 2hdc, (A) 6hdc, (G) 6hdc, (A) 6hdc, (I) 2hdc, (A) 2hdc, (J) 2hdc, (A) 2hdc, (H) 6hdc, (A) 2hdc, (G) 2hdc, (A) 2hdc, (G) 2hdc, (A) 2hdc, (H) 6hdc, (A) 2hdc, (J) 2hdc, (A) 2hdc, (I) 2hdc, (A) 6hdc, (G) 6hdc, (A) 6hdc, (H) 2hdc, (A) 2hdc, (J) 2hdc, (A) 2hdc, (I) 2hdc.

Rows 46 and 47: (I) Ch1, 2hdc, (A) 2hdc, (J) 2hdc, (A) 2hdc, (H) 6hdc, (A) 6hdc, (G) 6hdc, (A) 2hdc, (I) 2hdc, (A) 2hdc, (J) 2hdc, (A) 6hdc, (H) 2hdc, (A) 2hdc, (G) 2hdc, (A) 2hdc, (G) 2hdc, (A) 2hdc, (H) 2hdc, (A) 6hdc, (J) 2hdc, (A) 2hdc, (I) 2hdc, (A) 2hdc, (G) 6hdc, (A) 6hdc, (H) 6hdc, (A) 2hdc, (J) 2hdc, (A) 2hdc, (I) 2hdc.

Rows 48 and 49: (I) Ch1, 2hdc, (A) 2hdc, (J) 2hdc, (A) 6hdc, (H) 6hdc, (A) 6hdc, (G) 2hdc, (A) 2hdc, (I) 2hdc, (A) 2hdc, (J) 6hdc, (A) 2hdc, (H) 2hdc, (A) 2hdc, (G) 2hdc, (A) 2hdc, (G) 2hdc, (A) 2hdc, (H) 2hdc, (A) 2hdc, (J) 6hdc, (A) 2hdc, (I) 2hdc, (A) 2hdc, (G) 2hdc, (A) 6hdc, (H) 6hdc, (A) 6hdc, (J) 2hdc, (A) 2hdc, (I) 2hdc.

Rows 50 and 51: (I) Ch1, 2hdc, (A) 2hdc, (J) 6hdc, (A) 6hdc, (H) 6hdc, (A) 2hdc, (G) 2hdc, (A) 2hdc, (I) 2hdc, (A) 6hdc, (J) 2hdc, (A) 2hdc, (H) 2hdc, (A) 2hdc, (G) 2hdc, (A) 2hdc, (G) 2hdc, (A) 2hdc, (H) 2hdc, (A) 2hdc, (J) 2hdc, (A) 6hdc, (I) 2hdc, (A) 2hdc, (G) 2hdc, (A) 2hdc, (H) 6hdc, (A) 6hdc, (J) 6hdc, (A) 2hdc, (I) 2hdc.

Rows 52 and 53: (I) Ch1, 2hdc, (A) 6hdc, (J) 6hdc, (A) 6hdc, (H) 2hdc, (A) 2hdc, (G) 2hdc, (A) 2hdc, (I) 6hdc, (A) 2hdc, (J) 2hdc, (A) 2hdc, (H) 2hdc, (A) 2hdc, (G) 2hdc, (A) 2hdc, (G) 2hdc, (A) 2hdc, (H) 2hdc, (A) 2hdc, (J) 2hdc, (A) 2hdc, (I) 6hdc, (A) 2hdc, (G) 2hdc, (A) 2hdc, (H) 2hdc, (A) 6hdc, (J) 6hdc, (A) 6hdc, (I) 2hdc.

Rows 54 and 55: (I) Ch1, 6hdc, (A) 6hdc, (J) 6hdc, (A) 2hdc, (H) 2hdc, (A) 2hdc, (G) 2hdc, (A) 6hdc, (I) 2hdc, (A) 2hdc, (J) 2hdc, (A) 2hdc, (H) 2hdc, (A) 2hdc, (G) 2hdc, (A) 2hdc, (G) 2hdc, (A) 2hdc, (H) 2hdc, (A) 2hdc, (J) 2hdc, (A) 2hdc, (I) 2hdc, (A) 6hdc, (G) 2hdc, (A) 2hdc, (H) 2hdc, (A) 2hdc, (J) 6hdc, (A) 6hdc, (I) 6hdc.

Rows 56 and 57: (A) Ch1, 4hdc, (I) 6hdc, (A) 6hdc, (J) 2hdc, (A) 2hdc, (H) 2hdc, (A) 2hdc, (G) 6hdc, (A) 2hdc, (I) 2hdc, (A) 2hdc, (J) 2hdc, (A) 2hdc, (H) 2hdc, (A) 2hdc, (G) 2hdc, (A) 2hdc, (G) 2hdc, (A) 2hdc, (H) 2hdc, (A) 2hdc, (J) 2hdc, (A) 2hdc, (I) 2hdc, (A) 2hdc, (G) 6hdc, (A) 2hdc, (H) 2hdc, (A) 2hdc, (J) 2hdc, (A) 6hdc, (I) 6hdc, (A) 4hdc.

Rows 88 and 89: Repeat Rows 28 and 29.

Rows 90 and 91: Repeat Rows 26 and 27.

Rows 92 and 93: Repeat Rows 24 and 25.

Rows 94 and 95: Repeat Rows 22 and 23.

Rows 96 and 97: Repeat Rows 20 and 21.

Rows 98 and 99: Repeat Rows 18 and 19.

Rows 100 and 101: Repeat Rows 16 and 17.

Rows 102 and 103: Repeat Rows 14 and 15.

Rows 104 and 105: Repeat Rows 12 and 13.

Rows 106 and 107: Repeat Rows 10 and 11.

Rows 108 to 116: Repeat Rows 1 to 9.

Don't break yarn.

Row 117 (RS): (I) 94 sl sts across to the end.

Fasten off, and sew in all yarn ends.

Add tassels or pompoms if desired.

Rows 58 and 59: (A) Ch1, 8hdc, (I) 6hdc, (A) 2hdc, (J) 2hdc, (A) 2hdc, (H) 2hdc, (A) 6hdc, (G) 2hdc, (A) 2hdc, (I) 2hdc, (A) 2hdc, (J) 2hdc, (A) 2hdc, (H) 2hdc, (A) 2hdc, (G) 2hdc, (A) 2hdc, (G) 2hdc, (A) 2hdc, (H) 2hdc, (A) 2hdc, (J) 2hdc, (A) 2hdc, (I) 2hdc, (A) 2hdc, (G) 2hdc, (A) 6hdc, (H) 2hdc, (A) 2hdc, (J) 2hdc, (A) 2hdc, (I) 6hdc, (A) 8hdc.

Rows 60 and 61: Repeat Rows 56 and 57.

Rows 62 and 63: Repeat Rows 54 and 55.

Rows 64 and 65: Repeat Rows 52 and 53.

Rows 66 and 67: Repeat Rows 50 and 51.

Rows 68 and 69: Repeat Rows 48 and 49.

Rows 70 and 71: Repeat Rows 46 and 47.

Rows 72 and 73: Repeat Rows 44 and 45.

Rows 74 and 75: Repeat Rows 42 and 43.

Rows 76 and 77: Repeat Rows 40 and 41.

Rows 78 and 79: Repeat Rows 38 and 39.

Rows 80 and 81: Repeat Rows 36 and 37.

Rows 82 and 83: Repeat Rows 34 and 35.

Rows 84 and 85: Repeat Rows 32 and 33.

Rows 86 and 87: Repeat Rows 30 and 31.

WORKING FROM CHART

For each row, work all stitches from 1 to 94. Work Rows 1 to 116 once. Continue with Row 117 of written instructions.

KEY

☐ Buttercream Icing

▦ Mint Whoopie Pie

▦ Bubblegum Ice Cream

▦ French Blue Macaron

▦ Lavender Slice

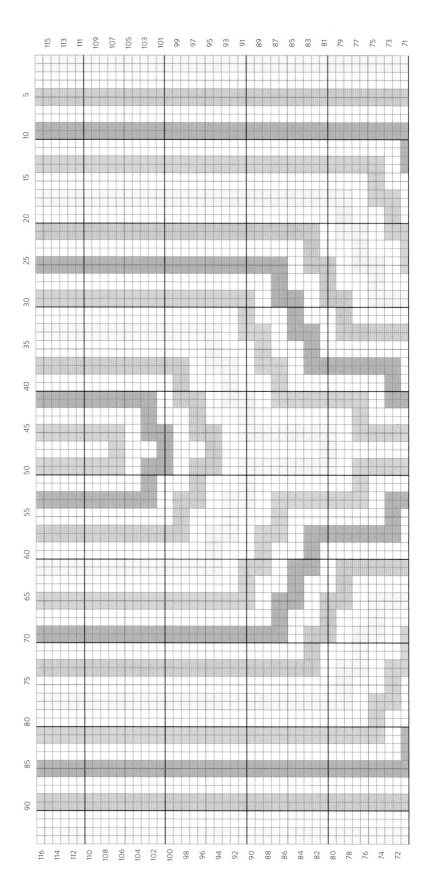

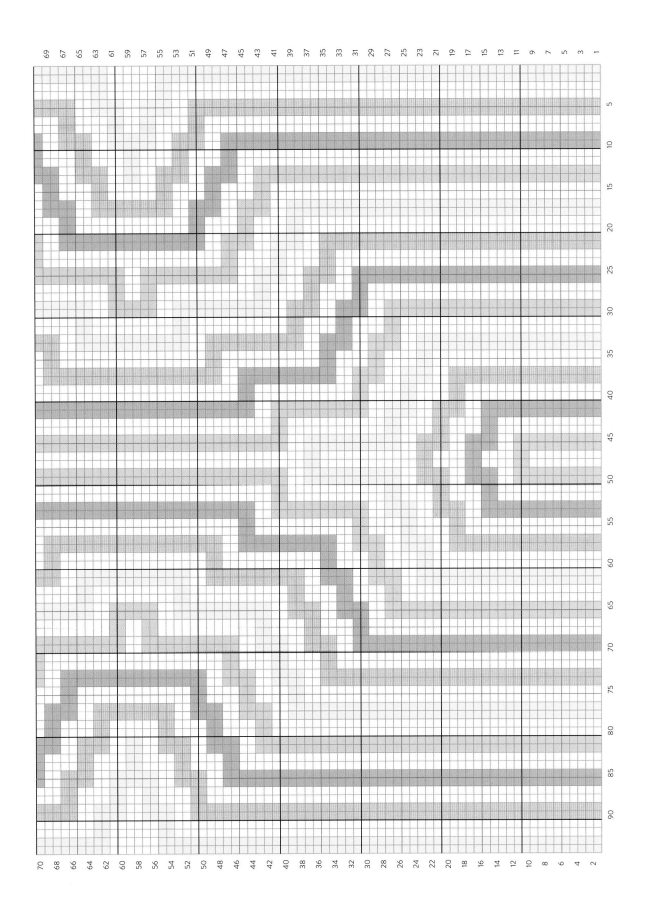

SECRET
STRIPES

A distortion seems to interrupt an orderly backdrop of stripes on this blanket. Look very closely and I am sure you will find the friendly message across the middle of this blanket!

YOU WILL NEED

HOOK

6.5mm (US K/10.5) hook

YARN

Scheepjes Truly Scrumptious (50% recycled polyester (recycled plastic bottles) and 50% acrylic), aran (worsted) weight, 100g (3½oz) = 108m (118yd), in the following shades:

- A: Buttercream Icing (302) x 6 balls
- C: Rose Barfi (321) x 2 balls
- H: Bubblegum Ice Cream (355) x 3 balls
- K: Sweet Potato Mochi (320) x 2 balls

YARN BALLS WOUND

- A: 12 x 50g (1¾oz)
- C: 4 x 50g (1¾oz)
- H: 6 x 50g (1¾oz)
- K: 4 x 50g (1¾oz)

TENSION (GAUGE)

11 stitches x 9 rows = 10cm (4in) square

FINISHED SIZE

126 x 88cm (49½ x 34½in)

PATTERN

Using a 6.5mm (US K/10.5) hook, chain 97 in Yarn A. Now start in the 2nd chain from the hook.

Rows 1 and 2: (A) Ch1, 96hdc. (96 sts)

Rows 3 and 4: (K) Ch1, (K) 96hdc.

Rows 5 and 6: (A) Ch1, 96hdc.

Rows 7 and 8: (H) Ch1, 96hdc.

Rows 9 and 10: (A) Ch1, 96hdc.

Rows 11 and 12: (C) Ch1, 96hdc.

Rows 13 to 24: Repeat Rows 1 to 12.

Row 25 (RS): (A) Ch1, 56hdc, (C) 2hdc, (A) 38hdc.

Row 26 (WS): (A) Ch1, 38hdc, (C) 2hdc, (A) 56hdc.

Row 27 (RS): (H) Ch1, 54hdc, (A) 2hdc, (C) 2hdc, (A) 2hdc, (H) 36hdc.

Row 28 (WS): (H) Ch1, 36hdc, (A) 2hdc, (C) 2hdc, (A) 2hdc, (H) 54hdc.

Row 29 (RS): (A) Ch1, 52hdc, (H) 2hdc, (A) 2hdc, (C) 2hdc, (A) 2hdc, (H) 2hdc, (A) 34hdc.

Row 30 (WS): (A) Ch1, 34hdc, (H) 2hdc, (A) 2hdc, (C) 2hdc, (A) 2hdc, (H) 2hdc, (A) 52hdc.

Row 31 (RS): (K) Ch1, 50hdc, (A) 2hdc, (H) 2hdc, (A) 2hdc, (C) 2hdc, (A) 2hdc, (H) 2hdc, (A) 2hdc, (K) 32hdc.

Row 32 (WS): Ch1, (K) 32hdc, (A) 2hdc, (H) 2hdc, (A) 2hdc, (C) 2hdc, (A) 2hdc, (H) 2hdc, (A) 2hdc, (K) 50hdc.

Row 33 (RS): (A) Ch1, 52hdc, (H) 2hdc, (A) 2hdc, (C) 2hdc, (A) 2hdc, (H) 2hdc, (A) 2hdc, (K) 2hdc, (A) 30hdc.

Row 34 (WS): (A) Ch1, 30hdc, (K) 2hdc, (A) 2hdc, (H) 2hdc, (A) 2hdc, (C) 2hdc, (A) 2hdc, (H) 2hdc, (A) 52hdc.

Row 35 (RS): (H) Ch1, 54hdc, (A) 2hdc, (C) 2hdc, (A) 2hdc, (H) 2hdc, (A) 2hdc, (K) 2hdc, (A) 2hdc, (H) 28hdc.

Row 36 (WS): (H) Ch1, 28hdc, (A) 2hdc, (K) 2hdc, (A) 2hdc, (H) 2hdc, (A) 2hdc, (C) 2hdc, (A) 2hdc, (H) 54hdc.

Row 37 (RS): (A) Ch1, 56hdc, (C) 2hdc, (A) 2hdc, (H) 2hdc, (A) 2hdc, (K) 2hdc, (A) 2hdc, (H) 2hdc, (A) 26hdc.

Row 38 (WS): (A) Ch1, 26hdc, (H) 2hdc, (A) 2hdc, (K) 2hdc, (A) 2hdc, (H) 2hdc, (A) 2hdc, (C) 2hdc, (A) 56hdc.

Row 39 (RS): (C) Ch1, 58hdc, (A) 2hdc, (H) 2hdc, (A) 2hdc, (K) 2hdc, (A) 2hdc, (H) 2hdc, (A) 2hdc, (C) 24hdc.

Row 40 (WS): (C) Ch1, 24hdc, (A) 2hdc, (H) 2hdc, (A) 2hdc, (K) 2hdc, (A) 2hdc, (H) 2hdc, (A) 2hdc, (C) 58hdc.

Row 41 (RS): (A) Ch1, 40hdc, (C) 2hdc, (A) 14hdc, (C) 2hdc, (A) 2hdc, (H) 2hdc, (A) 2hdc, (K) 2hdc, (A) 2hdc, (H) 2hdc, (A) 2hdc, (C) 2hdc, (A) 22hdc.

Row 42 (WS): (A) Ch1, 22hdc, (C) 2hdc, (A) 2hdc, (H) 2hdc, (A) 2hdc, (K) 2hdc, (A) 2hdc, (H) 2hdc, (A) 2hdc, (C) 2hdc, (A) 14hdc, (C) 2hdc, (A) 40hdc.

Row 43 (RS): (H) Ch1, 38hdc, (A) 2hdc, (C) 2hdc, (A) 2hdc, (H) 10hdc, (A) 2hdc, (C) 2hdc, (A) 2hdc, (H) 2hdc, (A) 2hdc, (K) 2hdc, (A) 2hdc, (H) 2hdc, (A) 2hdc, (C) 2hdc, (A) 2hdc, (H) 20hdc.

Row 44 (WS): (H) Ch1, 20hdc, (A) 2hdc, (C) 2hdc, (A) 2hdc, (H) 2hdc, (A) 2hdc, (K) 2hdc, (A) 2hdc, (H) 2hdc, (A) 2hdc, (C) 2hdc, (A) 2hdc, (H) 10hdc, (A) 2hdc, (C) 2hdc, (A) 2hdc, (H) 38hdc.

Row 45 (RS): (A) Ch1, 36hdc, (H) 2hdc, (A) 2hdc, (C) 2hdc, (A) 2hdc, (H) 2hdc, (A) 6hdc, (H) 2hdc, (A) 2hdc, (C) 2hdc, (A) 2hdc, (H) 2hdc, (A) 2hdc, (K) 2hdc, (A) 2hdc, (H) 2hdc, (A) 2hdc, (C) 2hdc, (A) 2hdc, (H) 2hdc, (A) 18hdc.

Row 46 (WS): (A) Ch1, 18hdc, (H) 2hdc, (A) 2hdc, (C) 2hdc, (A) 2hdc, (H) 2hdc, (A) 2hdc, (K) 2hdc, (A) 2hdc, (H) 2hdc, (A) 2hdc, (C) 2hdc, (A) 2hdc, (H) 2hdc, (A) 6hdc, (H) 2hdc, (A) 2hdc, (C) 2hdc, (A) 2hdc, (H) 2hdc, (A) 36hdc.

Row 47 (RS): (K) Ch1, 34hdc, (A) 2hdc, (H) 2hdc, (A) 2hdc, (C) 2hdc, (A) 2hdc, (H) 2hdc, (A) 2hdc, (K) 2hdc, (A) 2hdc, (H) 2hdc, (A) 2hdc, (C) 2hdc, (A) 2hdc, (H) 2hdc, (A) 2hdc, (K) 2hdc, (A) 2hdc, (H) 2hdc, (A) 2hdc, (C) 2hdc, (A) 2hdc, (H) 2hdc, (A) 2hdc, (K) 16hdc.

Row 48 (WS): (K) Ch1, 16hdc, (A) 2hdc, (H) 2hdc, (A) 2hdc, (C) 2hdc, (A) 2hdc, (H) 2hdc, (A) 2hdc, (K) 2hdc, (A) 2hdc, (H) 2hdc, (A) 2hdc, (C) 2hdc, (A) 2hdc, (H) 2hdc, (A) 2hdc, (K) 2hdc, (A) 2hdc, (H) 2hdc, (A) 2hdc, (C) 2hdc, (A) 2hdc, (H) 2hdc, (A) 2hdc, (K) 34hdc.

Row 49 (RS): (A) Ch1, 36hdc, (H) 2hdc, (A) 2hdc, (C) 2hdc, (A) 2hdc, (H) 2hdc, (A) 2hdc, (K) 2hdc, (A) 2hdc, (H) 2hdc, (A) 2hdc, (C) 2hdc, (A) 2hdc, (H) 2hdc, (A) 6hdc, (H) 2hdc, (A) 2hdc, (C) 2hdc, (A) 2hdc, (H) 2hdc, (A) 18hdc.

Row 50 (WS): (A) Ch1, 18hdc, (H) 2hdc, (A) 2hdc, (C) 2hdc, (A) 2hdc, (H) 2hdc, (A) 6hdc, (H) 2hdc, (A) 2hdc, (C) 2hdc, (A) 2hdc, (H) 2hdc, (A) 2hdc, (K) 2hdc, (A) 2hdc, (H) 2hdc, (A) 2hdc, (C) 2hdc, (A) 2hdc, (H) 2hdc, (A) 36hdc.

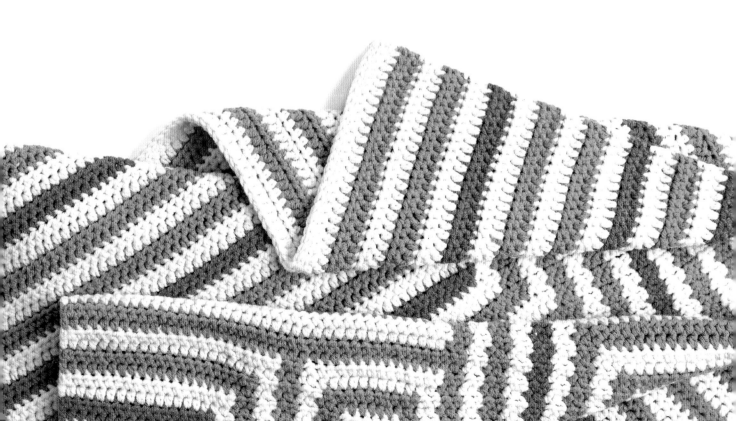

Row 51 (RS): (H) Ch1, 38hdc, (A) 2hdc, (C) 2hdc, (A) 2hdc, (H) 2hdc, (A) 2hdc, (K) 2hdc, (A) 2hdc, (H) 2hdc, (A) 2hdc, (C) 2hdc, (A) 2hdc, (H) 10hdc, (A) 2hdc, (C) 2hdc, (A) 2hdc, (H) 20hdc.

Row 52 (WS): (H) Ch1, 20hdc, (A) 2hdc, (C) 2hdc, (A) 2hdc, (H) 10hdc, (A) 2hdc, (C) 2hdc, (A) 2hdc, (H) 2hdc, (A) 2hdc, (K) 2hdc, (A) 2hdc, (H) 2hdc, (A) 2hdc, (C) 2hdc, (A) 2hdc, (H) 38hdc.

Row 53 (RS): (A) Ch1, 40hdc, (C) 2hdc, (A) 2hdc, (H) 2hdc, (A) 2hdc, (K) 2hdc, (A) 2hdc, (H) 2hdc, (A) 2hdc, (C) 2hdc, (A) 14hdc, (C) 2hdc, (A) 22hdc.

Row 54 (WS): (A) Ch1, 22hdc, (C) 2hdc, (A) 14hdc, (C) 2hdc, (A) 2hdc, (H) 2hdc, (A) 2hdc, (K) 2hdc, (A) 2hdc, (H) 2hdc, (A) 2hdc, (C) 2hdc, (A) 40hdc.

Row 55 (RS): (H) Ch1, 22hdc, (A) 2hdc, (C) 18hdc, (A) 2hdc, (H) 2hdc, (A) 2hdc, (K) 2hdc, (A) 2hdc, (H) 2hdc, (A) 2hdc, (C) 40hdc.

Row 56 (WS): (C) Ch1, 40hdc, (A) 2hdc, (H) 2hdc, (A) 2hdc, (K) 2hdc, (A) 2hdc, (H) 2hdc, (A) 2hdc, (C) 18hdc, (A) 2hdc, (H) 22hdc.

Row 57 (RS): (A) Ch1, (A) 20hdc, (H) 2hdc, (A) 2hdc, (C) 2hdc, (A) 18hdc, (H) 2hdc, (A) 2hdc, (K) 2hdc, (A) 2hdc, (H) 2hdc, (A) 2hdc, (C) 2hdc, (A) 38hdc.

Row 58 (WS): (A) Ch1, 38hdc, (C) 2hdc, (A) 2hdc, (H) 2hdc, (A) 2hdc, (K) 2hdc, (A) 2hdc, (H) 2hdc, (A) 18hdc, (C) 2hdc, (A) 2hdc, (H) 2hdc, (A) 20hdc.

Row 59 (RS): (K) Ch1, 18hdc, (A) 2hdc, (H) 2hdc, (A) 2hdc, (C) 2hdc, (A) 2hdc, (H) 18hdc, (A) 2hdc, (K) 2hdc, (A) 2hdc, (H) 2hdc, (A) 2hdc, (C) 2hdc, (A) 2hdc, (H) 36hdc.

Row 60 (WS): (H) Ch1, 36hdc, (A) 2hdc, (C) 2hdc, (A) 2hdc, (H) 2hdc, (A) 2hdc, (K) 2hdc, (A) 2hdc, (H) 18hdc, (A) 2hdc, (C) 2hdc, (A) 2hdc, (H) 2hdc, (A) 2hdc, (K) 18hdc.

Row 61 (RS): (A) Ch1, 16hdc, (K) 2hdc, (A) 2hdc, (H) 2hdc, (A) 2hdc, (C) 2hdc, (A) 2hdc, (H) 2hdc, (A) 18hdc, (K) 2hdc, (A) 2hdc, (H) 2hdc, (A) 2hdc, (C) 2hdc, (A) 2hdc, (H) 2hdc, (A) 34hdc.

Row 62 (WS): (A) Ch1, 34hdc, (H) 2hdc, (A) 2hdc, (C) 2hdc, (A) 2hdc, (H) 2hdc, (A) 2hdc, (K) 2hdc, (A) 18hdc, (H) 2hdc, (A) 2hdc, (C) 2hdc, (A) 2hdc, (H) 2hdc, (A) 2hdc, (K) 2hdc, (A) 16hdc.

Row 63 (RS): (C) Ch1, 14hdc, (A) 2hdc, (K) 2hdc, (A) 2hdc, (H) 2hdc, (A) 2hdc, (C) 2hdc, (A) 2hdc, (H) 2hdc, (A) 2hdc, (K) 18hdc, (A) 2hdc, (H) 2hdc, (A) 2hdc, (C) 2hdc, (A) 2hdc, (H) 2hdc, (A) 2hdc, (K) 32hdc.

Row 64 (WS): (K) Ch1, 32hdc, (A) 2hdc, (H) 2hdc, (A) 2hdc, (C) 2hdc, (A) 2hdc, (H) 2hdc, (A) 2hdc, (K) 18hdc, (A) 2hdc, (H) 2hdc, (A) 2hdc, (C) 2hdc, (A) 2hdc, (H) 2hdc, (A) 2hdc, (K) 2hdc, (A) 2hdc, (C) 14hdc.

Row 65 (RS): (A) Ch1, 16hdc, (K) 2hdc, (A) 2hdc, (H) 2hdc, (A) 2hdc, (C) 2hdc, (A) 2hdc, (H) 2hdc, (A) 2hdc, (K) 2hdc, (A) 18hdc, (H) 2hdc, (A) 2hdc, (C) 2hdc, (A) 2hdc, (H) 2hdc, (A) 34hdc.

Row 66 (WS): (A) Ch1, 34hdc, (H) 2hdc, (A) 2hdc, (C) 2hdc, (A) 2hdc, (H) 2hdc, (A) 18hdc, (K) 2hdc, (A) 2hdc, (H) 2hdc, (A) 2hdc, (C) 2hdc, (A) 2hdc, (H) 2hdc, (A) 2hdc, (K) 2hdc, (A) 16hdc.

Row 67 (RS): (K) Ch1, 18hdc, (A) 2hdc, (H) 2hdc, (A) 2hdc, (C) 2hdc, (A) 2hdc, (H) 2hdc, (A) 2hdc, (K) 2hdc, (A) 2hdc, (H) 18hdc, (A) 2hdc, (C) 2hdc, (A) 2hdc, (H) 36hdc.

Row 68 (WS): (H) Ch1, 36hdc, (A) 2hdc, (C) 2hdc, (A) 2hdc, (H) 18hdc, (A) 2hdc, (K) 2hdc, (A) 2hdc, (H) 2hdc, (A) 2hdc, (C) 2hdc, (A) 2hdc, (H) 2hdc, (A) 2hdc, (K) 18hdc.

Row 69 (RS): (A) Ch1, 20hdc, (H) 2hdc, (A) 2hdc, (C) 2hdc, (A) 2hdc, (H) 2hdc, (A) 2hdc, (K) 2hdc, (A) 2hdc, (H) 2hdc, (A) 18hdc, (C) 2hdc, (A) 38hdc.

Row 70 (WS): (A) Ch1, 38hdc, (C) 2hdc, (A) 18hdc, (H) 2hdc, (A) 2hdc, (K) 2hdc, (A) 2hdc, (H) 2hdc, (A) 2hdc, (C) 2hdc, (A) 2hdc, (H) 2hdc, (A) 20hdc.

Row 71 (RS): (H) Ch1, 22hdc, (A) 2hdc, (C) 2hdc, (A) 2hdc, (H) 2hdc, (A) 2hdc, (K) 2hdc, (A) 2hdc, (H) 2hdc, (A) 2hdc, (C) 56hdc.

Row 72 (WS): (C) Ch1, 56hdc, (A) 2hdc, (H) 2hdc, (A) 2hdc, (K) 2hdc, (A) 2hdc, (H) 2hdc, (A) 2hdc, (C) 2hdc, (A) 2hdc, (H) 22hdc.

Row 73 (RS): (A) Ch1, 24hdc, (C) 2hdc, (A) 2hdc, (H) 2hdc, (A) 2hdc, (K) 2hdc, (A) 2hdc, (H) 2hdc, (A) 2hdc, (C) 2hdc, (A) 54hdc.

Row 74 (WS): (A) Ch1, 54hdc, (C) 2hdc, (A) 2hdc, (H) 2hdc, (A) 2hdc, (K) 2hdc, (A) 2hdc, (H) 2hdc, (A) 2hdc, (C) 2hdc, (A) 24hdc.

Row 75 (RS): (C) Ch1, 26hdc, (A) 2hdc, (H) 2hdc, (A) 2hdc, (K) 2hdc, (A) 2hdc, (H) 2hdc, (A) 2hdc, (C) 2hdc, (A) 2hdc, (H) 52hdc.

Row 76 (WS): (H) Ch1, 52hdc, (A) 2hdc, (C) 2hdc, (A) 2hdc, (H) 2hdc, (A) 2hdc, (K) 2hdc, (A) 2hdc, (H) 2hdc, (A) 2hdc, (C) 26hdc.

Row 77 (RS): (A) Ch1, 28hdc, (H) 2hdc, (A) 2hdc, (K) 2hdc, (A) 2hdc, (H) 2hdc, (A) 2hdc, (C) 2hdc, (A) 2hdc, (H) 2hdc, (A) 50hdc.

Row 78 (WS): (A) Ch1, 50hdc, (H) 2hdc, (A) 2hdc, (C) 2hdc, (A) 2hdc, (H) 2hdc, (A) 2hdc, (K) 2hdc, (A) 2hdc, (H) 2hdc, (A) 28hdc.

Row 79 (RS): (H) Ch1, 30hdc, (A) 2hdc, (K) 2hdc, (A) 2hdc, (H) 2hdc, (A) 2hdc, (C) 2hdc, (A) 2hdc, (H) 2hdc, (A) 2hdc, (K) 48hdc.

Row 80 (WS): (K) Ch1, 48hdc, (A) 2hdc, (H) 2hdc, (A) 2hdc, (C) 2hdc, (A) 2hdc, (H) 2hdc, (A) 2hdc, (K) 2hdc, (A) 2hdc, (H) 30hdc.

Row 81 (RS): (A) Ch1, 32hdc, (K) 2hdc, (A) 2hdc, (H) 2hdc, (A) 2hdc, (C) 2hdc, (A) 2hdc, (H) 2hdc, (A) 50hdc.

Row 82 (WS): (A) Ch1, 50hdc, (H) 2hdc, (A) 2hdc, (C) 2hdc, (A) 2hdc, (H) 2hdc, (A) 2hdc, (K) 2hdc, (A) 32hdc.

Row 83 (RS): (K) Ch1, 34hdc, (A) 2hdc, (H) 2hdc, (A) 2hdc, (C) 2hdc, (A) 2hdc, (H) 52hdc.

Row 84 (WS): (H) Ch1, 52hdc, (A) 2hdc, (C) 2hdc, (A) 2hdc, (H) 2hdc, (A) 2hdc, (K) 34hdc.

Row 85 (RS): (A) Ch1, 36hdc, (H) 2hdc, (A) 2hdc, (C) 2hdc, (A) 54hdc.

Row 86 (WS): (A) Ch1, 54hdc, (C) 2hdc, (A) 2hdc, (H) 2hdc, (A) 36hdc.

Row 87 (RS): (H) Ch1, 38hdc, (A) 2hdc, (C) 56hdc.

Row 88 (WS): (C) Ch1, 56hdc, (A) 2hdc, (H) 38hdc.

Rows 89 to 112: Repeat Rows 1 to 12 twice.

Rows 113 and 114: (A) Ch1, 96hdc.

Don't break yarn.

Row 115 (RS): (A) 96 sl sts across to the end.

Fasten off, and sew in all yarn ends.

Add tassels or pompoms if desired.

TIP

Always check the number of small yarn balls in each colour you'll need for your blanket before you start, and prepare them in advance. This will help you so much when adding yarns to your blanket as you go; preparation is the key.

WORKING FROM CHART

For each row, work all stitches from 1 to 96. Work Rows 1 to 88 once, then repeat Rows 1 to 12 twice more. Continue with Rows 113 to 115 of written instructions.

KEY

☐ Buttercream Icing

▧ Rose Barfi

▧ Bubblegum Ice Cream

▧ Sweet Potato Mochi

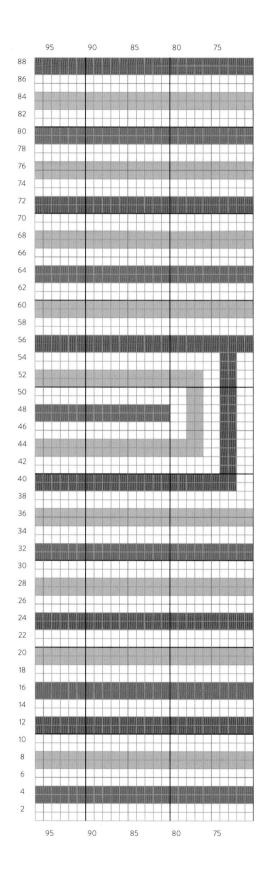

RADIANT ZIGZAGS

On this blanket, zigzags radiate in to a central point that culminates in a pink square surrounded by yellow lines. The yellow lines then stretch out to the edges of the blanket forming a cross shape.

YOU WILL NEED

HOOK

6.5mm (US K/10.5) hook

YARN

Scheepjes Truly Scrumptious (50% recycled polyester (recycled plastic bottles) and 50% acrylic), aran (worsted) weight, 100g (3½oz) = 108m (118yd), in the following shades:

- A: Buttercream Icing (302) x 6 balls
- B: Cotton Candy Meringue (330) x 2 balls
- E: Custard Pie (341) x 2 balls
- F: Pistachio Bundt Cake (318) x 2 balls
- H: Bubblegum Ice Cream (355) x 2 balls

YARN BALLS WOUND

- A: 16 x 37g (1¼oz)
- B: 3 x 66g (2⅓oz)
- E: 4 x 50g (1¾oz)
- F: 4 x 50g (1¾oz)
- H: 4 x 50g (1¾oz)

TENSION (GAUGE)

11 stitches x 9 rows = 10cm (4in) square

FINISHED SIZE

119 x 87cm (47 x 34in)

PATTERN

Using a 6.5mm (US K/10.5) hook, chain 97 in Yarn A. Now start in the 2nd chain from the hook.

Rows 1 to 4: (A) Ch1, 19hdc, (H) 2hdc, (A) 2hdc, (F) 2hdc, (A) 2hdc, (E) 2hdc, (A) 2hdc, (B) 2hdc, (A) 2hdc, (H) 2hdc, (A) 2hdc, (F) 2hdc, (A) 2hdc, (E) 2hdc, (A) 2hdc, (B) 2hdc, (A) 2hdc, (E) 2hdc, (A) 2hdc, (F) 2hdc, (A) 2hdc, (H) 2hdc, (A) 2hdc, (B) 2hdc, (A) 2hdc, (E) 2hdc, (A) 2hdc, (F) 2hdc, (A) 2hdc, (H) 2hdc, (A) 19hdc. (96 sts)

Rows 5 to 8: (H) Ch1, (H) 21hdc, (A) 2hdc, (F) 2hdc, (A) 2hdc, (E) 2hdc, (A) 2hdc, (B) 2hdc, (A) 2hdc, (H) 2hdc, (A) 2hdc, (F) 2hdc, (A) 2hdc, (E) 2hdc, (A) 2hdc, (B) 2hdc, (A) 2hdc, (E) 2hdc, (A) 2hdc, (F) 2hdc, (A) 2hdc, (H) 2hdc, (A) 2hdc, (B) 2hdc, (A) 2hdc, (E) 2hdc, (A) 2hdc, (F) 2hdc, (A) 2hdc, (H) 21hdc.

Rows 9 to 12: (A) Ch1, 23hdc, (F) 2hdc, (A) 2hdc, (E) 2hdc, (A) 2hdc, (B) 2hdc, (A) 2hdc, (H) 2hdc, (A) 2hdc, (F) 2hdc, (A) 2hdc, (E) 2hdc, (A) 2hdc, (B) 2hdc, (A) 2hdc, (E) 2hdc, (A) 2hdc, (F) 2hdc, (A) 2hdc, (H) 2hdc, (A) 2hdc, (B) 2hdc, (A) 2hdc, (E) 2hdc, (A) 2hdc, (F) 2hdc, (A) 23hdc.

Rows 13 to 16: (A) Ch1, 2hdc, (F) 23hdc, (A) 2hdc, (E) 2hdc, (A) 2hdc, (B) 2hdc, (A) 2hdc, (H) 2hdc, (A) 2hdc, (F) 2hdc, (A) 2hdc, (E) 2hdc, (A) 2hdc, (B) 2hdc, (A) 2hdc, (E) 2hdc, (A) 2hdc, (F) 2hdc, (A) 2hdc, (H) 2hdc, (A) 2hdc, (B) 2hdc, (A) 2hdc, (E) 2hdc, (A) 2hdc, (F) 23hdc, (A) 2hdc.

Rows 17 to 20: (A) Ch1, 2hdc, (F) 4hdc, (A) 21hdc, (E) 2hdc, (A) 2hdc, (B) 2hdc, (A) 2hdc, (H) 2hdc, (A) 2hdc, (F) 2hdc, (A) 2hdc, (E) 2hdc, (A) 2hdc, (B) 2hdc, (A) 2hdc, (E) 2hdc, (A) 2hdc, (F) 2hdc, (A) 2hdc, (H) 2hdc, (A) 2hdc, (B) 2hdc, (A) 2hdc, (E) 2hdc, (A) 21hdc, (F) 4hdc, (A) 2hdc.

Rows 21 to 24: (A) Ch1, 2hdc, (F) 4hdc, (A) 4hdc, (E) 19hdc, (A) 2hdc, (B) 2hdc, (A) 2hdc, (H) 2hdc, (A) 2hdc, (F) 2hdc, (A) 2hdc, (E) 2hdc, (A) 2hdc, (B) 2hdc, (A) 2hdc, (E) 2hdc, (A) 2hdc, (F) 2hdc, (A) 2hdc, (H) 2hdc, (A) 2hdc, (B) 2hdc, (A) 2hdc, (E) 19hdc, (A) 4hdc, (F) 4hdc, (A) 2hdc.

Rows 25 to 28: (A) Ch1, 2hdc, (F) 4hdc, (A) 4hdc, (E) 4hdc, (A) 17hdc, (B) 2hdc, (A) 2hdc, (H) 2hdc, (A) 2hdc, (F) 2hdc, (A) 2hdc, (E) 2hdc, (A) 2hdc, (B) 2hdc, (A) 2hdc, (E) 2hdc, (A) 2hdc, (F) 2hdc, (A) 2hdc, (H) 2hdc, (A) 2hdc, (B) 2hdc, (A) 17hdc, (E) 4hdc, (A) 4hdc, (F) 4hdc, (A) 2hdc.

Rows 29 to 32: (A) Ch1, 2hdc, (F) 4hdc, (A) 4hdc, (E) 4hdc, (A) 4hdc, (B) 15hdc, (A) 2hdc, (H) 2hdc, (A) 2hdc, (F) 2hdc, (A) 2hdc, (E) 2hdc, (A) 2hdc, (B) 2hdc, (A) 2hdc, (E) 2hdc, (A) 2hdc, (F) 2hdc, (A) 2hdc, (H) 2hdc, (A) 2hdc, (B) 15hdc, (A) 4hdc, (E) 4hdc, (A) 4hdc, (F) 4hdc, (A) 2hdc.

Rows 33 and 34: (A) Ch1, 2hdc, (F) 4hdc, (A) 4hdc, (E) 4hdc, (A) 4hdc, (B) 4hdc, (A) 13hdc, (H) 2hdc, (A) 2hdc, (F) 2hdc, (A) 2hdc, (E) 2hdc, (A) 2hdc, (B) 2hdc, (A) 2hdc, (E) 2hdc, (A) 2hdc, (F) 2hdc, (A) 2hdc, (H) 2hdc, (A) 13hdc, (B) 4hdc, (A) 4hdc, (E) 4hdc, (A) 4hdc, (F) 4hdc, (A) 2hdc.

Rows 35 and 36: (F) Ch1, 6hdc, (A) 4hdc, (E) 4hdc, (A) 4hdc, (B) 4hdc, (A) 13hdc, (H) 2hdc, (A) 2hdc, (F) 2hdc, (A) 2hdc, (E) 2hdc, (A) 2hdc, (B) 2hdc, (A) 2hdc, (E) 2hdc, (A) 2hdc, (F) 2hdc, (A) 2hdc, (H) 2hdc, (A) 13hdc, (B) 4hdc, (A) 4hdc, (E) 4hdc, (A) 4hdc, (F) 6hdc.

Rows 37 and 38: (A) Ch1, 10hdc, (E) 4hdc, (A) 4hdc, (B) 4hdc, (A) 4hdc, (H) 11hdc, (A) 2hdc, (F) 2hdc, (A) 2hdc, (E) 2hdc, (A) 2hdc, (B) 2hdc, (A) 2hdc, (E) 2hdc, (A) 2hdc, (F) 2hdc, (A) 2hdc, (H) 11hdc, (A) 4hdc, (B) 4hdc, (A) 4hdc, (E) 4hdc, (A) 10hdc.

Rows 39 and 40: (E) Ch1, 14hdc, (A) 4hdc, (B) 4hdc, (A) 4hdc, (H) 11hdc, (A) 2hdc, (F) 2hdc, (A) 2hdc, (E) 2hdc, (A) 2hdc, (B) 2hdc, (A) 2hdc, (E) 2hdc, (A) 2hdc, (F) 2hdc, (A) 2hdc, (H) 11hdc, (A) 4hdc, (B) 4hdc, (A) 4hdc, (E) 14hdc.

Rows 41 and 42: (A) Ch1, 18hdc, (B) 4hdc, (A) 4hdc, (H) 4hdc, (A) 9hdc, (F) 2hdc, (A) 2hdc, (E) 2hdc, (A) 2hdc, (B) 2hdc, (A) 2hdc, (E) 2hdc, (A) 2hdc, (F) 2hdc, (A) 9hdc, (H) 4hdc, (A) 4hdc, (B) 4hdc, (A) 18hdc.

Rows 43 and 44: (B) Ch1, 22hdc, (A) 4hdc, (H) 4hdc, (A) 9hdc, (F) 2hdc, (A) 2hdc, (E) 2hdc, (A) 2hdc, (B) 2hdc, (A) 2hdc, (E) 2hdc, (A) 2hdc, (F) 2hdc, (A) 9hdc, (H) 4hdc, (A) 4hdc, (B) 22hdc.

Rows 45 to 48: (A) Ch1, 26hdc, (H) 4hdc, (A) 4hdc, (F) 7hdc, (A) 2hdc, (E) 2hdc, (A) 2hdc, (B) 2hdc, (A) 2hdc, (E) 2hdc, (A) 2hdc, (F) 7hdc, (A) 4hdc, (H) 4hdc, (A) 26hdc.

Rows 49 and 50: (H) Ch1, 30hdc, (A) 4hdc, (F) 4hdc, (A) 5hdc, (E) 2hdc, (A) 2hdc, (B) 2hdc, (A) 2hdc, (E) 2hdc, (A) 5hdc, (F) 4hdc, (A) 4hdc, (H) 30hdc.

Rows 51 and 52: (A) Ch1, 34hdc, (F) 4hdc, (A) 2hdc, (E) 5hdc, (A) 2hdc, (B) 2hdc, (A) 2hdc, (E) 5hdc, (A) 2hdc, (F) 4hdc, (A) 34hdc.

Rows 53 and 54: (F) Ch1, 38hdc, (A) 2hdc, (E) 2hdc, (A) 5hdc, (B) 2hdc, (A) 5hdc, (E) 2hdc, (A) 2hdc, (F) 38hdc.

Rows 55 and 56: (A) Ch1, 40hdc, (E) 2hdc, (A) 2hdc, (B) 8hdc, (A) 2hdc, (E) 2hdc, (A) 40hdc.

Rows 57 and 58: (E) Ch1, 42hdc, (A) 2hdc, (B) 2hdc, (A) 4hdc, (B) 2hdc, (A) 2hdc, (E) 42hdc.

Rows 59 and 60: Repeat Rows 55 and 56.

Rows 61 and 62: Repeat Rows 53 and 54.

Rows 63 and 64: Repeat Rows 51 and 52.

Rows 65 and 66: Repeat Rows 49 and 50.

Rows 67 to 70: Repeat Rows 45 to 48.

Rows 71 and 72: Repeat Rows 43 and 44.

Rows 73 and 74: Repeat Rows 41 and 42.

Rows 75 and 76: Repeat Rows 39 and 40.

Rows 77 and 78: Repeat Rows 37 and 38.

Rows 79 and 80: Repeat Rows 35 and 36.

Rows 81 and 82: Repeat Rows 33 and 34.

Rows 83 to 86: Repeat Rows 29 to 32.

Rows 87 to 90: Repeat Rows 25 to 28.

Rows 91 to 94: Repeat Rows 21 to 24.

Rows 95 to 98: Repeat Rows 17 to 20.

Rows 99 to 102: Repeat Rows 13 to 16.

Rows 103 to 106: Repeat Rows 9 to 12.

Rows 107 to 110: Repeat Rows 5 to 8.

Rows 111 to 114: Repeat Rows 1 to 4.

Don't break yarn.

Row 115 (RS): (A) 96 sl sts across to the end.

Fasten off, and sew in all yarn ends.

Add tassels or pompoms if desired.

WORKING FROM CHART

For each row, work all stitches from
1 to 96. Work Rows 1 to 114 once.
Continue with Row 115 of written
instructions.

KEY

☐ Buttercream Icing

▦ Cotton Candy Meringue

▦ Custard Pie

▦ Pistachio Bundt Cake

▦ Bubblegum Ice Cream

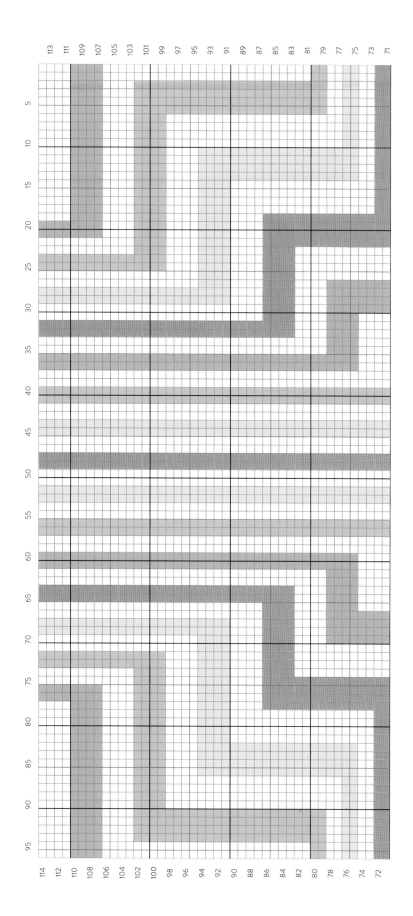

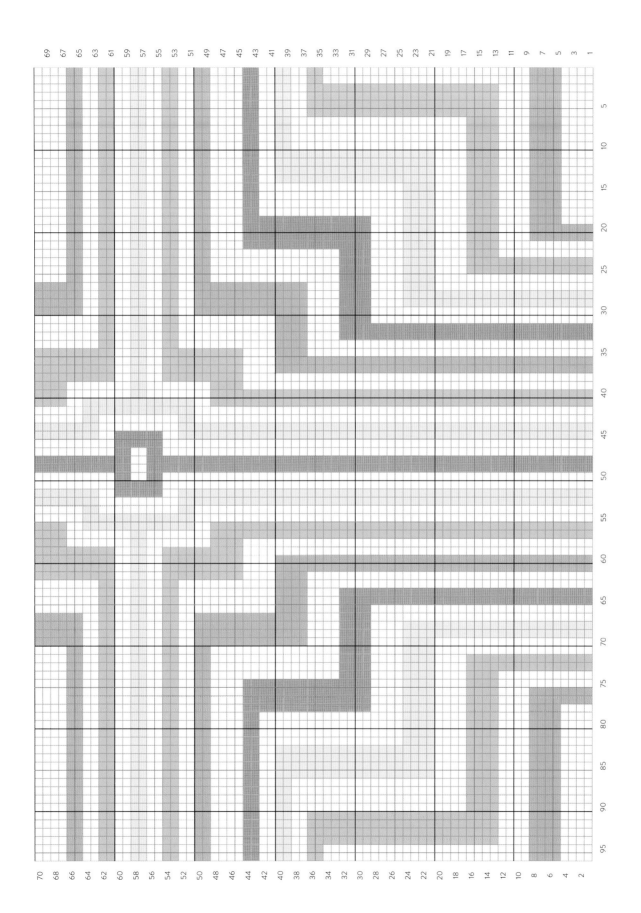

DREAMY LAYERS

In this design, four light-tinted, rainbow-coloured squares appear to sit on top of a vertical swathe of lines, which themselves sit between two rectangles. The simple elements combine to create a complex look.

YOU WILL NEED

HOOK

6.5mm (US K/10.5) hook

YARN

Scheepjes Truly Scrumptious (50% recycled polyester (recycled plastic bottles) and 50% acrylic), aran (worsted) weight, 100g (3½oz) = 108m (118yd), in the following shades:

- A: Buttercream Icing (302) x 8 balls
- B: Cotton Candy Meringue (330) x 2 balls
- D: Orange Cheesecake (332) x 2 balls
- E: Custard Pie (341) x 2 balls
- F: Pistachio Bundt Cake (318) x 2 balls
- I: French Blue Macaron (343) x 2 balls
- J: Lavender Slice (334) x 2 balls

YARN BALLS WOUND

- A: 32 x 25g (⅞oz)
- B: 4 x 50g (1¾oz)
- D: 4 x 50g (1¾oz)
- E: 6 x 33g (1⅛oz)
- F: 6 x 33g (1⅛oz)
- I: 6 x 33g (1⅛oz)
- J: 5 x 40g (1⅜oz)

TENSION

11 stitches x 9 rows = 10cm (4in) square

FINISHED SIZE

126 x 110cm (49½ x 43½in)

PATTERN

Using a 6.5mm (US K/10.5) hook, chain 127 in Yarn A. Now start in the 2nd chain from the hook.

Rows 1 and 2: (A) Ch1, (A) 54hdc, (D) 2hdc, (A) 2hdc, (B) 2hdc, (A) 2hdc, (J) 2hdc, (A) 2hdc, (B) 2hdc, (A) 2hdc, (D) 2hdc, (A) 54hdc. (126 sts)

Rows 3 and 4: (A) Ch1, 2hdc, (E) 50hdc, (A) 2hdc, (D) 2hdc, (A) 2hdc, (B) 2hdc, (A) 2hdc, (J) 2hdc, (A) 2hdc, (B) 2hdc, (A) 2hdc, (D) 2hdc, (A) 2hdc, (E) 50hdc, (A) 2hdc.

Rows 5 and 6: (A) Ch1, 2hdc, (E) 2hdc, (A) 46hdc, (E) 2hdc, (A) 2hdc, (D) 2hdc, (A) 2hdc, (B) 2hdc, (A) 2hdc, (J) 2hdc, (A) 2hdc, (B) 2hdc, (A) 2hdc, (D) 2hdc, (A) 2hdc, (E) 2hdc, (A) 46hdc, (E) 2hdc, (A) 2hdc.

Rows 7 and 8: (A) Ch1, 2hdc, (E) 2hdc, (A) 2hdc, (F) 42hdc, (A) 2hdc, (E) 2hdc, (A) 2hdc, (D) 2hdc, (A) 2hdc, (B) 2hdc, (A) 2hdc, (J) 2hdc, (A) 2hdc, (B) 2hdc, (A) 2hdc, (D) 2hdc, (A) 2hdc, (E) 2hdc, (A) 2hdc, (F) 42hdc, (A) 2hdc, (E) 2hdc, (A) 2hdc.

Rows 9 and 10: (A) Ch1, 2hdc, (E) 2hdc, (A) 2hdc, (F) 2hdc, (A) 38hdc, (F) 2hdc, (A) 2hdc, (E) 2hdc, (A) 2hdc, (D) 2hdc, (A) 2hdc, (B) 2hdc, (A) 2hdc, (J) 2hdc, (A) 2hdc, (B) 2hdc, (A) 2hdc, (D) 2hdc, (A) 2hdc, (E) 2hdc, (A) 2hdc, (F) 2hdc, (A) 38hdc, (F) 2hdc, (A) 2hdc, (E) 2hdc, (A) 2hdc.

Rows 11 and 12: (A) Ch1, 2hdc, (E) 2hdc, (A) 2hdc, (F) 2hdc, (A) 2hdc, (I) 34hdc, (A) 2hdc, (F) 2hdc, (A) 2hdc, (E) 2hdc, (A) 2hdc, (D) 2hdc, (A) 2hdc, (B) 2hdc, (A) 2hdc, (J) 2hdc, (A) 2hdc, (B) 2hdc, (A) 2hdc, (D) 2hdc, (A) 2hdc, (E) 2hdc, (A) 2hdc, (F) 2hdc, (A) 2hdc, (I) 34hdc, (A) 2hdc, (F) 2hdc, (A) 2hdc, (E) 2hdc, (A) 2hdc.

Rows 13 and 14: (A) Ch1, 2hdc, (E) 2hdc, (A) 2hdc, (F) 2hdc, (A) 2hdc, (I) 2hdc, (A) 30hdc, (I) 2hdc, (A) 2hdc, (F) 2hdc, (A) 2hdc, (E) 2hdc, (A) 2hdc, (D) 2hdc, (A) 2hdc, (B) 2hdc, (A) 2hdc, (J) 2hdc, (A) 2hdc, (B) 2hdc, (A) 2hdc, (D) 2hdc, (A) 2hdc, (E) 2hdc, (A) 2hdc, (F) 2hdc, (A) 2hdc, (I) 2hdc, (A) 30hdc, (I) 2hdc, (A) 2hdc, (F) 2hdc, (A) 2hdc, (E) 2hdc, (A) 2hdc.

Rows 15 and 16: (A) Ch1, 2hdc, (E) 2hdc, (A) 2hdc, (F) 2hdc, (A) 2hdc, (I) 2hdc, (A) 2hdc, (J) 98hdc, (A) 2hdc, (I) 2hdc, (A) 2hdc, (F) 2hdc, (A) 2hdc, (E) 2hdc, (A) 2hdc.

Rows 17 and 18: (A) Ch1, 2hdc, (E) 2hdc, (A) 2hdc, (F) 2hdc, (A) 2hdc, (I) 2hdc, (A) 2hdc, (J) 2hdc, (A) 46hdc, (J) 2hdc, (A) 46hdc, (J) 2hdc, (A) 2hdc, (I) 2hdc, (A) 2hdc, (F) 2hdc, (A) 2hdc, (E) 2hdc, (A) 2hdc.

Rows 19 and 20: (A) Ch1, 2hdc, (E) 2hdc, (A) 2hdc, (F) 2hdc, (A) 2hdc, (I) 2hdc, (A) 2hdc, (J) 2hdc, (A) 2hdc, (B) 42hdc, (A) 2hdc, (J) 2hdc, (A) 2hdc, (B) 42hdc, (A) 2hdc, (J) 2hdc, (A) 2hdc, (I) 2hdc, (A) 2hdc, (F) 2hdc, (A) 2hdc, (E) 2hdc, (A) 2hdc.

Rows 21 and 22: (A) Ch1, 2hdc, (E) 2hdc, (A) 2hdc, (F) 2hdc, (A) 2hdc, (I) 2hdc, (A) 2hdc, (J) 2hdc, (A) 2hdc, (B) 2hdc, (A) 38hdc, (B) 2hdc, (A) 2hdc, (J) 2hdc, (A) 2hdc, (B) 2hdc, (A) 38hdc, (B) 2hdc, (A) 2hdc, (J) 2hdc, (A) 2hdc, (I) 2hdc, (A) 2hdc, (F) 2hdc, (A) 2hdc, (E) 2hdc, (A) 2hdc.

Rows 23 and 24: (A) Ch1, 2hdc, (E) 2hdc, (A) 2hdc, (F) 2hdc, (A) 2hdc, (I) 2hdc, (A) 2hdc, (J) 2hdc, (A) 2hdc, (B) 2hdc, (A) 2hdc, (D) 34hdc, (A) 2hdc, (B) 2hdc, (A) 2hdc, (J) 2hdc, (A) 2hdc, (B) 2hdc, (A) 2hdc, (D) 34hdc, (A) 2hdc, (B) 2hdc, (A) 2hdc, (J) 2hdc, (A) 2hdc, (I) 2hdc, (A) 2hdc, (F) 2hdc, (A) 2hdc, (E) 2hdc, (A) 2hdc.

Rows 25 and 26: (A) Ch1, 2hdc, (E) 2hdc, (A) 2hdc, (F) 2hdc, (A) 2hdc, (I) 2hdc, (A) 2hdc, (J) 2hdc, (A) 2hdc, (B) 2hdc, (A) 2hdc, (D) 2hdc, (A) 30hdc, (D) 2hdc, (A) 2hdc, (B) 2hdc, (A) 2hdc, (J) 2hdc, (A) 2hdc, (B) 2hdc, (A) 2hdc, (D) 2hdc, (A) 30hdc, (D) 2hdc, (A) 2hdc, (B) 2hdc, (A) 2hdc, (J) 2hdc, (A) 2hdc, (I) 2hdc, (A) 2hdc, (F) 2hdc, (A) 2hdc, (E) 2hdc, (A) 2hdc.

Rows 27 and 28: (A) Ch1, 2hdc, (E) 2hdc, (A) 2hdc, (F) 2hdc, (A) 2hdc, (I) 2hdc, (A) 2hdc, (J) 2hdc, (A) 2hdc, (B) 2hdc, (A) 2hdc, (D) 2hdc, (A) 2hdc, (E) 26hdc, (A) 2hdc, (D) 2hdc, (A) 2hdc, (B) 2hdc, (A) 2hdc, (J) 2hdc, (A) 2hdc, (B) 2hdc, (A) 2hdc, (D) 2hdc, (A) 2hdc, (E) 26hdc, (A) 2hdc, (D) 2hdc, (A) 2hdc, (B) 2hdc, (A) 2hdc, (J) 2hdc, (A) 2hdc, (I) 2hdc, (A) 2hdc, (F) 2hdc, (A) 2hdc, (E) 2hdc, (A) 2hdc.

Rows 29 and 30: (A) Ch1, 2hdc, (E) 2hdc, (A) 2hdc, (F) 2hdc, (A) 2hdc, (I) 2hdc, (A) 2hdc, (J) 2hdc, (A) 2hdc, (B) 2hdc, (A) 2hdc, (D) 2hdc, (A) 2hdc, (E) 2hdc, (A) 22hdc, (E) 2hdc, (A) 2hdc, (D) 2hdc, (A) 2hdc, (B) 2hdc, (A) 2hdc, (J) 2hdc, (A) 2hdc, (B) 2hdc, (A) 2hdc, (D) 2hdc, (A) 2hdc, (E) 2hdc, (A) 22hdc, (E) 2hdc, (A) 2hdc, (D) 2hdc, (A) 2hdc, (B) 2hdc, (A) 2hdc, (J) 2hdc, (A) 2hdc, (I) 2hdc, (A) 2hdc, (F) 2hdc, (A) 2hdc, (E) 2hdc, (A) 2hdc.

Rows 31 and 32: (A) Ch1, 2hdc, (E) 2hdc, (A) 2hdc, (F) 2hdc, (A) 2hdc, (I) 2hdc, (A) 2hdc, (J) 2hdc, (A) 2hdc, (B) 2hdc, (A) 2hdc, (D) 2hdc, (A) 2hdc, (E) 2hdc, (A) 2hdc, (F) 18hdc, (A) 2hdc, (E) 2hdc, (A) 2hdc, (D) 2hdc, (A) 2hdc, (B) 2hdc, (A) 2hdc, (J) 2hdc, (A) 2hdc, (B) 2hdc, (A) 2hdc, (D) 2hdc, (A) 2hdc, (E) 2hdc, (A) 2hdc, (F) 18hdc, (A) 2hdc, (E) 2hdc, (A) 2hdc, (D) 2hdc, (A) 2hdc, (B) 2hdc, (A) 2hdc, (J) 2hdc, (A) 2hdc, (I) 2hdc, (A) 2hdc, (F) 2hdc, (A) 2hdc, (E) 2hdc, (A) 2hdc.

Rows 33 and 34: (A) Ch1, 2hdc, (E) 2hdc, (A) 2hdc, (F) 2hdc, (A) 2hdc, (I) 2hdc, (A) 2hdc, (J) 2hdc, (A) 2hdc, (B) 2hdc, (A) 2hdc, (D) 2hdc, (A) 2hdc, (E) 2hdc, (A) 2hdc, (F) 2hdc, (A) 14hdc, (F) 2hdc, (A) 2hdc, (E) 2hdc, (A) 2hdc, (D) 2hdc, (A) 2hdc, (B) 2hdc, (A) 2hdc, (J) 2hdc, (A) 2hdc, (B) 2hdc, (A) 2hdc, (D) 2hdc, (A) 2hdc, (E) 2hdc, (A) 2hdc, (F) 2hdc, (A) 14hdc, (F) 2hdc, (A) 2hdc, (E) 2hdc, (A) 2hdc, (D) 2hdc, (A) 2hdc, (B) 2hdc, (A) 2hdc, (J) 2hdc, (A) 2hdc, (I) 2hdc, (A) 2hdc, (F) 2hdc, (A) 2hdc, (E) 2hdc, (A) 2hdc.

Rows 35 and 36: (A) Ch1, 2hdc, (E) 2hdc, (A) 2hdc, (F) 2hdc, (A) 2hdc, (I) 2hdc, (A) 2hdc, (J) 2hdc, (A) 2hdc, (B) 2hdc, (A) 2hdc, (D) 2hdc, (A) 2hdc, (E) 2hdc, (A) 2hdc, (F) 2hdc, (A) 2hdc, (I) 10hdc, (A) 2hdc, (F) 2hdc, (A) 2hdc, (E) 2hdc, (A) 2hdc, (D) 2hdc, (A) 2hdc, (B) 2hdc, (A) 2hdc, (J) 2hdc, (A) 2hdc, (B) 2hdc, (A) 2hdc, (D) 2hdc, (A) 2hdc, (E) 2hdc, (A) 2hdc, (F) 2hdc, (A) 2hdc, (I) 10hdc, (A) 2hdc, (F) 2hdc, (A) 2hdc, (E) 2hdc, (A) 2hdc, (D) 2hdc, (A) 2hdc, (B) 2hdc, (A) 2hdc, (J) 2hdc, (A) 2hdc, (I) 2hdc, (A) 2hdc, (F) 2hdc, (A) 2hdc, (E) 2hdc, (A) 2hdc.

Rows 37 and 38: (A) Ch1, 2hdc, (E) 2hdc, (A) 2hdc, (F) 2hdc, (A) 2hdc, (I) 2hdc, (A) 2hdc, (J) 2hdc, (A) 2hdc, (B) 2hdc, (A) 2hdc, (D) 2hdc, (A) 2hdc, (E) 2hdc, (A) 2hdc, (F) 2hdc, (A) 2hdc, (I) 2hdc, (A) 6hdc, (I) 2hdc, (A) 2hdc, (F) 2hdc, (A) 2hdc, (E) 2hdc, (A) 2hdc, (D) 2hdc, (A) 2hdc, (B) 2hdc, (A) 2hdc, (J) 2hdc, (A) 2hdc, (B) 2hdc, (A) 2hdc, (D) 2hdc, (A) 2hdc, (E) 2hdc, (A) 2hdc, (F) 2hdc, (A) 2hdc, (I) 2hdc, (A) 6hdc, (I) 2hdc, (A) 2hdc, (F) 2hdc, (A) 2hdc, (E) 2hdc, (A) 2hdc, (D) 2hdc, (A) 2hdc, (B) 2hdc, (A) 2hdc, (J) 2hdc, (A) 2hdc, (I) 2hdc, (A) 2hdc, (F) 2hdc, (A) 2hdc, (E) 2hdc, (A) 2hdc.

Rows 39 and 40: (A) Ch1, 2hdc, (E) 2hdc, (A) 2hdc, (F) 2hdc, (A) 2hdc, (I) 2hdc, (A) 2hdc, (J) 2hdc, (A) 2hdc, (B) 2hdc, (A) 2hdc, (D) 2hdc, (A) 2hdc, (E) 2hdc, (A) 2hdc, (F) 2hdc, (A) 2hdc, (I) 2hdc, (A) 2hdc, (J) 2hdc, (A) 2hdc, (I) 2hdc, (A) 2hdc, (F) 2hdc, (A) 2hdc, (E) 2hdc, (A) 2hdc, (D) 2hdc, (A) 2hdc, (B) 2hdc, (A) 2hdc, (J) 2hdc, (A) 2hdc, (B) 2hdc, (A) 2hdc, (D) 2hdc, (A) 2hdc, (E) 2hdc, (A) 2hdc, (F) 2hdc, (A) 2hdc, (I) 2hdc, (A) 2hdc, (J) 2hdc, (A) 2hdc, (I) 2hdc, (A) 2hdc, (F) 2hdc, (A) 2hdc, (E) 2hdc, (A) 2hdc, (D) 2hdc, (A) 2hdc, (B) 2hdc, (A) 2hdc, (J) 2hdc, (A) 2hdc, (I) 2hdc, (A) 2hdc, (F) 2hdc, (A) 2hdc, (E) 2hdc, (A) 2hdc.

Rows 41 and 42: Repeat Rows 37 and 38.

Rows 43 and 44: Repeat Rows 35 and 36.

Rows 45 and 46: Repeat Rows 33 and 34.

Rows 47 and 48: Repeat Rows 31 and 32.

Rows 49 and 50: Repeat Rows 29 and 30.

Rows 51 and 52: Repeat Rows 27 and 28.

Rows 53 and 54: Repeat Rows 25 and 26.

Rows 55 and 56: Repeat Rows 23 and 24.

Rows 57 and 58: Repeat Rows 21 and 22.

Rows 59 and 60: Repeat Rows 19 and 20.

Rows 61 and 62: Repeat Rows 17 and 18.

Rows 63 to 110: Repeat Rows 15 to 62.

Rows 111 and 112: Repeat Rows 15 and 16.

Rows 113 and 114: Repeat Rows 13 and 14.

Rows 115 and 116: Repeat Rows 11 and 12.

Rows 117 and 118: Repeat Rows 9 and 10.

Rows 119 and 120: Repeat Rows 7 and 8.

Rows 121 and 122: Repeat Rows 5 and 6.

Rows 123 and 124: Repeat Rows 3 and 4.

Rows 125 and 126: Repeat Rows 1 and 2.

Don't break yarn.

Row 127 (RS): (A) 126 sl sts across to the end.

Fasten off, and sew in all yarn ends.

Add tassels or pompoms if desired.

WORKING FROM CHART

For each row, work all stitches from 1 to 126. First work Chart A Rows 1 to 62 once, then Rows 15 to 62 once more, then Rows 15 and 16 once again. Continue on to Chart B, work Rows 113 to 126 once. Continue with Row 127 of written instructions.

CHART A

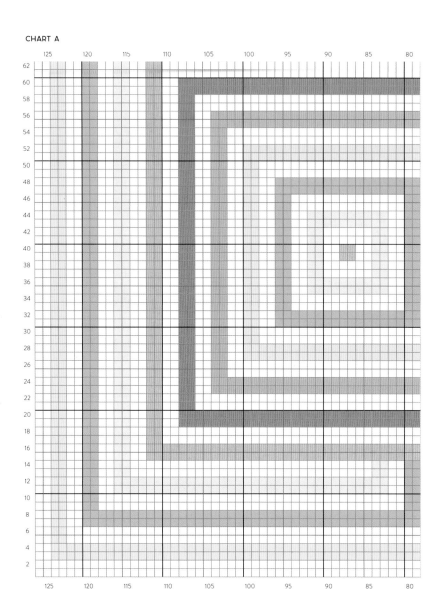

CHART B

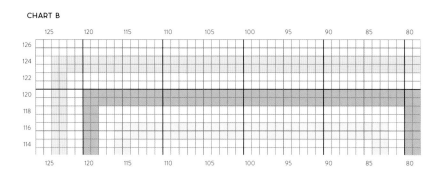

KEY

- ☐ Buttercream Icing
- ▧ Orange Cheesecake
- ▧ Pistachio Bundt Cake
- ▧ Lavender Slice
- ▧ Cotton Candy Meringue
- ▧ Custard Pie
- ▧ French Blue Macaron

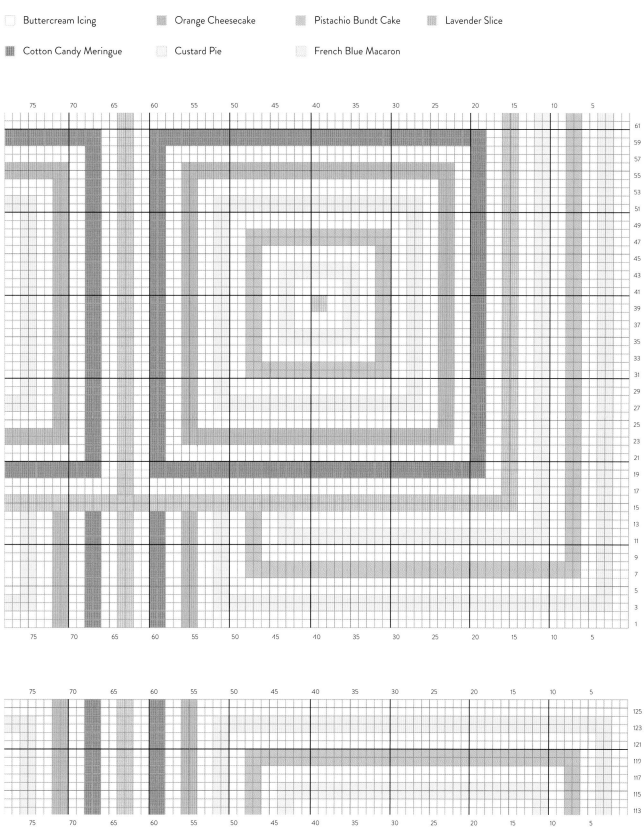

PLUS POSITIVE

By shifting the alignment of simple lines of block colour, this pattern design creates a plus shape that seems to project forwards from the background of concentric squares.

YOU WILL NEED

HOOK

6.5mm (US K/10.5) hook

YARN

Scheepjes Truly Scrumptious (50% recycled polyester (recycled plastic bottles) and 50% acrylic), aran (worsted) weight, 100g (3½oz) = 108m (118yd), in the following shades:

- A: Buttercream Icing (302) x 7 balls
- C: Rose Barfi (321) x 1 ball
- D: Orange Cheesecake (332) x 1 ball
- E: Custard Pie (341) x 1 ball
- F: Pistachio Bundt Cake (318) x 2 balls
- I: French Blue Macaron (343) x 2 balls
- J: Lavender Slice (334) x 2 balls

YARN BALLS WOUND

- A: 14 x 50g (1¾oz)
- C: 5 x 20g (¾oz)
- D: 3 x 33g (1⅛oz)
- E: 3 x 33g (1⅛oz)
- F: 3 x 66g (2⅓oz)
- I: 3 x 66g (2⅓oz)
- J: 3 x 66g (2⅓oz)

TENSION (GAUGE)

11 stitches x 9 rows = 10cm (4in) square

FINISHED SIZE

127 x 102cm (50 x 40in)

PATTERN

Using a 6.5mm (US K/10.5) hook, chain 117 in Yarn A. Now start in the 2nd chain from the hook.

Rows 1 to 4: (A) Ch1, 48hdc, (C) 20hdc, (A) 48hdc. (116 sts)

Rows 5 to 8: (A) Ch1, 4hdc, (J) 44hdc, (A) 20hdc, (J) 44hdc, (A) 4hdc.

Rows 9 to 12: (A) Ch1, 4hdc, (J) 4hdc, (A) 40hdc, (J) 20hdc, (A) 40hdc, (J) 4hdc, (A) 4hdc.

Rows 13 to 16: (A) Ch1, 4hdc, (J) 4hdc, (A) 4hdc, (I) 36hdc, (A) 20hdc, (I) 36hdc, (A) 4hdc, (J) 4hdc, (A) 4hdc.

Rows 17 to 20: (A) Ch1, 4hdc, (J) 4hdc, (A) 4hdc, (I) 4hdc, (A) 32hdc, (I) 20hdc, (A) 32hdc, (I) 4hdc, (A) 4hdc, (J) 4hdc, (A) 4hdc.

Rows 21 to 24: (A) Ch1, 4hdc, (J) 4hdc, (A) 4hdc, (I) 4hdc, (A) 4hdc, (F) 28hdc, (A) 20hdc, (F) 28hdc, (A) 4hdc, (I) 4hdc, (A) 4hdc, (J) 4hdc, (A) 4hdc.

Rows 25 to 28: (A) Ch1, 4hdc, (J) 4hdc, (A) 4hdc, (I) 4hdc, (A) 4hdc, (F) 4hdc, (A) 24hdc, (F) 20hdc, (A) 24hdc, (F) 4hdc, (A) 4hdc, (I) 4hdc, (A) 4hdc, (J) 4hdc, (A) 4hdc.

Rows 29 to 32: (A) Ch1, 4hdc, (J) 4hdc, (A) 4hdc, (I) 4hdc, (A) 4hdc, (F) 4hdc, (A) 4hdc, (E) 20hdc, (A) 20hdc, (E) 20hdc, (A) 4hdc, (F) 4hdc, (A) 4hdc, (I) 4hdc, (A) 4hdc, (J) 4hdc, (A) 4hdc.

Rows 33 to 36: (A) Ch1, 4hdc, (J) 4hdc, (A) 4hdc, (I) 4hdc, (A) 4hdc, (F) 4hdc, (A) 4hdc, (E) 4hdc, (A) 16hdc, (E) 20hdc, (A) 16hdc, (E) 4hdc, (A) 4hdc, (F) 4hdc, (A) 4hdc, (I) 4hdc, (A) 4hdc, (J) 4hdc, (A) 4hdc.

Rows 37 to 40: (A) Ch1, 4hdc, (J) 4hdc, (A) 4hdc, (I) 4hdc, (A) 4hdc, (F) 4hdc, (A) 4hdc, (E) 4hdc, (A) 4hdc, (D) 12hdc, (A) 20hdc, (D) 12hdc, (A) 4hdc, (E) 4hdc, (A) 4hdc, (F) 4hdc, (A) 4hdc, (I) 4hdc, (A) 4hdc, (J) 4hdc, (A) 4hdc.

Rows 41 to 44: (A) Ch1, 4hdc, (J) 4hdc, (A) 4hdc, (I) 4hdc, (A) 4hdc, (F) 4hdc, (A) 4hdc, (E) 4hdc, (A) 4hdc, (D) 4hdc, (A) 8hdc, (D) 20hdc, (A) 8hdc, (D) 4hdc, (A) 4hdc, (E) 4hdc, (A) 4hdc, (F) 4hdc, (A) 4hdc, (I) 4hdc, (A) 4hdc, (J) 4hdc, (A) 4hdc.

Rows 45 to 48: (A) Ch1, 4hdc, (J) 4hdc, (A) 4hdc, (I) 4hdc, (A) 4hdc, (F) 4hdc, (A) 4hdc, (E) 4hdc, (A) 4hdc, (D) 4hdc, (A) 4hdc, (C) 4hdc, (A) 20hdc, (C) 4hdc, (A) 4hdc, (D) 4hdc, (A) 4hdc, (E) 4hdc, (A) 4hdc, (F) 4hdc, (A) 4hdc, (I) 4hdc, (A) 4hdc, (J) 4hdc, (A) 4hdc.

Rows 49 to 52: (C) Ch1, 4hdc, (A) 4hdc, (J) 4hdc, (A) 4hdc, (I) 4hdc, (A) 4hdc, (F) 4hdc, (A) 4hdc, (E) 4hdc, (A) 4hdc, (D) 4hdc, (A) 4hdc, (C) 20hdc, (A) 4hdc, (D) 4hdc, (A) 4hdc, (E) 4hdc, (A) 4hdc, (F) 4hdc, (A) 4hdc, (I) 4hdc, (A) 4hdc, (J) 4hdc, (A) 4hdc, (C) 4hdc.

Rows 53 to 56: (C) Ch1, 4hdc, (A) 4hdc, (J) 4hdc, (A) 4hdc, (I) 4hdc, (A) 4hdc, (F) 4hdc, (A) 4hdc, (E) 4hdc, (A) 4hdc, (D) 4hdc, (A) 4hdc, (C) 4hdc, (A) 12hdc, (C) 4hdc, (A) 4hdc, (D) 4hdc, (A) 4hdc, (E) 4hdc, (A) 4hdc, (F) 4hdc, (A) 4hdc, (I) 4hdc, (A) 4hdc, (J) 4hdc, (A) 4hdc, (C) 4hdc.

Rows 57 to 60: (C) Ch1, 4hdc, (A) 4hdc, (J) 4hdc, (A) 4hdc, (I) 4hdc, (A) 4hdc, (F) 4hdc, (A) 4hdc, (E) 4hdc, (A) 4hdc, (D) 4hdc, (A) 4hdc, (C) 4hdc, (A) 4hdc, (C) 4hdc, (A) 4hdc, (C) 4hdc, (A) 4hdc, (D) 4hdc, (A) 4hdc, (E) 4hdc, (A) 4hdc, (F) 4hdc, (A) 4hdc, (I) 4hdc, (A) 4hdc, (J) 4hdc, (A) 4hdc, (C) 4hdc.

Rows 61 to 64: Repeat Rows 53 to 56.

Rows 65 to 68: Repeat Rows 49 to 52.

Rows 69 to 72: Repeat Rows 45 to 48.

Rows 73 to 76: Repeat Rows 41 to 44.

Rows 77 to 80: Repeat Rows 37 to 40.

Rows 81 to 84: Repeat Rows 33 to 36.

Rows 85 to 88: Repeat Rows 29 to 32.

Rows 89 to 92: Repeat Rows 25 to 28.

Rows 93 to 96: Repeat Rows 21 to 24.

Rows 97 to 100: Repeat Rows 17 to 20.

Rows 101 to 104: Repeat Rows 13 to 16.

Rows 105 to 108: Repeat Rows 9 to 12.

Rows 109 to 112: Repeat Rows 5 to 8.

Rows 113 to 116: Repeat Rows 1 to 4.

Don't break yarn.

Row 117 (RS): (A) 116 sl sts across to the end.

Fasten off, and sew in all yarn ends.

Add tassels or pompoms if desired.

TIP

You could make the blanket using the written pattern alone, or just follow the chart. Both methods are useful and are even better when used together. Just use the method that best works for you.

WORKING FROM CHART

For each row, work all stitches from 1 to 116. Work Rows 1 to 116 ~~~~ Continue with Row 117 of written instructions.

KEY

- ☐ Buttercream Icing
- ▦ Rose Barfi
- ▦ Orange Cheesecake
- ▦ Custard Pie
- ▦ Pistachio Bundt Cake
- ☐ French Blue Macaron
- ▦ Lavender Slice

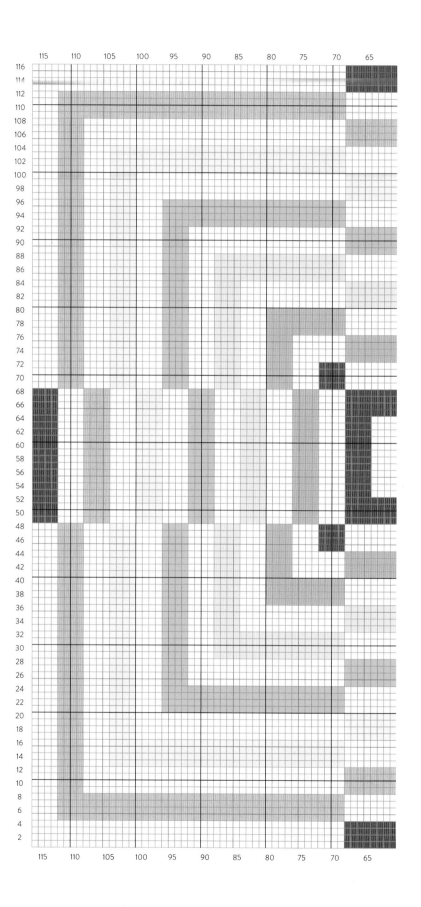

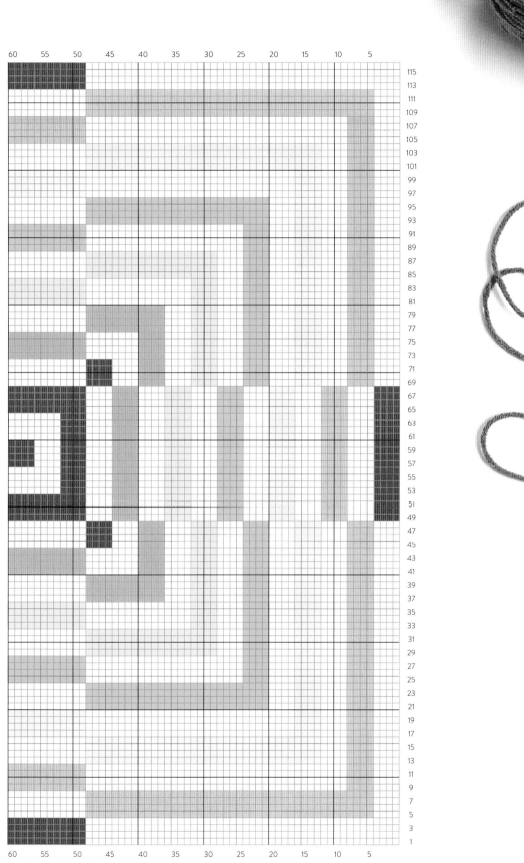

CENTRE POINT

The green, blue and pink lines that make up this pattern all point towards the centre of the blanket, but to add extra interest they are distorted into an ellipse shape before they get there.

YOU WILL NEED

HOOK

6.5mm (US K/10.5) hook

YARN

Scheepjes Truly Scrumptious (50% recycled polyester (recycled plastic bottles) and 50% acrylic), aran (worsted) weight, 100g (3½oz) = 108m (118yd), in the following shades:

- A: Buttercream Icing (302) x 6 balls
- B: Cotton Candy Meringue (330) x 2 balls
- G: Mint Whoopie Pie (340) x 3 balls
- H: Bubblegum Ice Cream (355) x 2 balls

YARN BALLS WOUND

- A: 26 x 23g (¾oz)
- B: 8 x 25g (⅞oz)
- G: 10 x 30g (1oz)
- H: 9 x 22g (¾oz)

TENSION (GAUGE)

11 stitches x 9 rows = 10cm (4in) square

FINISHED SIZE

119 x 94cm (47 x 37in)

PATTERN

Using a 6.5mm (US K/10.5) hook, chain 111 in Yarn H. Now start in the 2nd chain from the hook.

Rows 1 to 6: (H) Ch1, 2hdc, (A) 2hdc, (G) 2hdc, (A) 2hdc, (B) 2hdc, (A) 2hdc, (H) 2hdc, (A) 2hdc, (G) 2hdc, (A) 2hdc, (B) 2hdc, (A) 2hdc, (H) 2hdc, (A) 2hdc, (G) 2hdc, (A) 2hdc, (B) 2hdc, (A) 2hdc, (H) 2hdc, (A) 2hdc, (G) 2hdc, (A) 4hdc, (B) 2hdc, (A) 2hdc, (G) 2hdc, (A) 2hdc, (H) 2hdc, (A) 2hdc, (G) 2hdc, (A) 2hdc, (B) 2hdc, (A) 4hdc, (G) 2hdc, (A) 2hdc, (H) 2hdc, (A) 2hdc, (B) 2hdc, (A) 2hdc, (G) 2hdc, (A) 2hdc, (H) 2hdc, (A) 2hdc, (B) 2hdc, (A) 2hdc, (G) 2hdc, (A) 2hdc, (H) 2hdc, (A) 2hdc, (B) 2hdc, (A) 2hdc, (G) 2hdc, (A) 2hdc, (H) 2hdc. (110 sts)

Rows 7 and 8: (A) Ch1, 4hdc, (G) 2hdc, (A) 2hdc, (B) 2hdc, (A) 2hdc, (H) 2hdc, (A) 2hdc, (G) 2hdc, (A) 2hdc, (B) 2hdc, (A) 2hdc, (H) 2hdc, (A) 2hdc, (G) 2hdc, (A) 2hdc, (B) 2hdc, (A) 2hdc, (H) 2hdc, (A) 2hdc, (G) 2hdc, (A) 4hdc, (B) 2hdc, (A) 2hdc, (G) 2hdc, (A) 2hdc, (H) 2hdc, (A) 2hdc, (G) 2hdc, (A) 2hdc, (B) 2hdc, (A) 4hdc, (G) 2hdc, (A) 2hdc, (H) 2hdc, (A) 2hdc, (B) 2hdc, (A) 2hdc, (G) 2hdc, (A) 2hdc, (H) 2hdc, (A) 2hdc, (B) 2hdc, (A) 2hdc, (G) 2hdc, (A) 2hdc, (H) 2hdc, (A) 2hdc, (B) 2hdc, (A) 2hdc, (G) 2hdc, (A) 4hdc.

Rows 9 and 10: (G) Ch1, 6hdc, (A) 2hdc, (B) 2hdc, (A) 2hdc, (H) 2hdc, (A) 2hdc, (G) 2hdc, (A) 2hdc, (B) 2hdc, (A) 2hdc, (H) 2hdc, (A) 2hdc, (G) 2hdc, (A) 2hdc, (B) 2hdc, (A) 2hdc, (H) 2hdc, (A) 2hdc, (G) 2hdc, (A) 4hdc, (B) 2hdc, (A) 2hdc, (G) 2hdc, (A) 2hdc, (H) 2hdc, (A) 2hdc, (G) 2hdc, (A) 2hdc, (B) 2hdc, (A) 4hdc, (G) 2hdc, (A) 2hdc, (H) 2hdc, (A) 2hdc, (B) 2hdc, (A) 2hdc, (G) 2hdc, (A) 2hdc, (H) 2hdc, (A) 2hdc, (B) 2hdc, (A) 2hdc, (G) 2hdc, (A) 2hdc, (H) 2hdc, (A) 2hdc, (B) 2hdc, (A) 2hdc, (G) 6hdc.

Rows 11 and 12: (A) Ch1, 8hdc, (B) 2hdc, (A) 2hdc, (H) 2hdc, (A) 2hdc, (G) 2hdc, (A) 2hdc, (B) 2hdc, (A) 2hdc, (H) 2hdc, (A) 2hdc, (G) 2hdc, (A) 2hdc, (B) 2hdc, (A) 2hdc, (H) 2hdc, (A) 2hdc, (G) 2hdc, (A) 4hdc, (B) 2hdc, (A) 2hdc, (G) 2hdc, (A) 2hdc, (H) 2hdc, (A) 2hdc, (G) 2hdc, (A) 2hdc, (B) 2hdc, (A) 4hdc, (G) 2hdc, (A) 2hdc, (H) 2hdc, (A) 2hdc, (B) 2hdc, (A) 2hdc, (G) 2hdc, (A) 2hdc, (H) 2hdc, (A) 2hdc, (B) 2hdc, (A) 2hdc, (G) 2hdc, (A) 2hdc, (H) 2hdc, (A) 2hdc, (B) 2hdc, (A) 8hdc.

Rows 13 and 14: (B) Ch1, 10hdc, (A) 2hdc, (H) 2hdc, (A) 2hdc, (G) 2hdc, (A) 2hdc, (B) 2hdc, (A) 2hdc, (H) 2hdc, (A) 2hdc, (G) 2hdc, (A) 2hdc, (B) 2hdc, (A) 2hdc, (H) 2hdc, (A) 2hdc, (G) 2hdc, (A) 4hdc, (B) 2hdc, (A) 2hdc, (G) 2hdc, (A) 2hdc, (H) 2hdc, (A) 2hdc, (G) 2hdc, (A) 2hdc, (B) 2hdc, (A) 4hdc, (G) 2hdc, (A) 2hdc, (H) 2hdc, (A) 2hdc, (B) 2hdc, (A) 2hdc, (G) 2hdc, (A) 2hdc, (H) 2hdc, (A) 2hdc, (B) 2hdc, (A) 2hdc, (G) 2hdc, (A) 2hdc, (H) 2hdc, (A) 2hdc, (B) 10hdc.

Rows 15 and 16: (A) Ch1, 12hdc, (H) 2hdc, (A) 2hdc, (G) 2hdc, (A) 2hdc, (B) 2hdc, (A) 2hdc, (H) 2hdc, (A) 2hdc, (G) 2hdc, (A) 2hdc, (B) 2hdc, (A) 2hdc, (H) 2hdc, (A) 2hdc, (G) 2hdc, (A) 4hdc, (B) 2hdc, (A) 2hdc, (G) 2hdc, (A) 2hdc, (H) 2hdc, (A) 2hdc, (G) 2hdc, (A) 2hdc, (B) 2hdc, (A) 4hdc, (G) 2hdc, (A) 2hdc, (H) 2hdc, (A) 2hdc, (B) 2hdc, (A) 2hdc, (G) 2hdc, (A) 2hdc, (H) 2hdc, (A) 12hdc.

Rows 17 and 18: (H) Ch1, 14hdc, (A) 2hdc, (G) 2hdc, (A) 2hdc, (B) 2hdc, (A) 2hdc, (H) 2hdc, (A) 2hdc, (G) 2hdc, (A) 2hdc, (B) 2hdc, (A) 2hdc, (H) 2hdc, (A) 2hdc, (G) 2hdc, (A) 4hdc, (B) 2hdc, (A) 2hdc, (G) 2hdc, (A) 2hdc, (H) 2hdc, (A) 2hdc, (G) 2hdc, (A) 2hdc, (B) 2hdc, (A) 4hdc, (G) 2hdc, (A) 2hdc, (H) 2hdc, (A) 2hdc, (B) 2hdc, (A) 2hdc, (G) 2hdc, (A) 2hdc, (H) 2hdc, (A) 2hdc, (B) 2hdc, (A) 2hdc, (G) 2hdc, (A) 2hdc, (H) 14hdc.

Rows 19 and 20: (A) Ch1, 16hdc, (G) 2hdc, (A) 2hdc, (B) 2hdc, (A) 2hdc, (H) 2hdc, (A) 2hdc, (G) 2hdc, (A) 2hdc, (B) 2hdc, (A) 2hdc, (H) 2hdc, (A) 2hdc, (G) 2hdc, (A) 4hdc, (B) 2hdc, (A) 2hdc, (G) 2hdc, (A) 2hdc, (H) 2hdc, (A) 2hdc, (G) 2hdc, (A) 2hdc, (B) 2hdc, (A) 4hdc, (G) 2hdc, (A) 2hdc, (H) 2hdc, (A) 2hdc, (B) 2hdc, (A) 2hdc, (G) 2hdc, (A) 2hdc, (H) 2hdc, (A) 2hdc, (B) 2hdc, (A) 2hdc, (G) 2hdc, (A) 16hdc.

Rows 21 and 22: (G) Ch1, 18hdc, (A) 2hdc, (B) 2hdc, (A) 2hdc, (H) 2hdc, (A) 2hdc, (G) 2hdc, (A) 2hdc, (B) 2hdc, (A) 2hdc, (H) 2hdc, (A) 2hdc, (G) 2hdc, (A) 4hdc, (B) 2hdc, (A) 2hdc, (G) 2hdc, (A) 2hdc, (H) 2hdc, (A) 2hdc, (G) 2hdc, (A) 2hdc, (B) 2hdc, (A) 4hdc, (G) 2hdc, (A) 2hdc, (H) 2hdc, (A) 2hdc, (B) 2hdc, (A) 2hdc, (G) 2hdc, (A) 2hdc, (H) 2hdc, (A) 2hdc, (B) 2hdc, (A) 2hdc, (G) 18hdc.

Rows 23 and 24: (A) Ch1, 20hdc, (B) 2hdc, (A) 2hdc, (H) 2hdc, (A) 2hdc, (G) 2hdc, (A) 2hdc, (B) 2hdc, (A) 2hdc, (H) 2hdc, (A) 2hdc, (G) 2hdc, (A) 4hdc, (B) 2hdc, (A) 2hdc, (G) 2hdc, (A) 6hdc, (G) 2hdc, (A) 2hdc, (B) 2hdc, (A) 4hdc, (G) 2hdc, (A) 2hdc, (H) 2hdc, (A) 2hdc, (B) 2hdc, (A) 2hdc, (G) 2hdc, (A) 2hdc, (H) 2hdc, (A) 2hdc, (B) 2hdc, (A) 20hdc.

Rows 25 and 26: (B) Ch1, 22hdc, (A) 2hdc, (H) 2hdc, (A) 2hdc, (G) 2hdc, (A) 2hdc, (B) 2hdc, (A) 2hdc, (H) 2hdc, (A) 2hdc, (G) 2hdc, (A) 4hdc, (B) 2hdc, (A) 2hdc, (G) 4hdc, (A) 2hdc, (G) 4hdc, (A) 2hdc, (B) 2hdc, (A) 4hdc, (G) 2hdc, (A) 2hdc, (H) 2hdc, (A) 2hdc, (B) 2hdc, (A) 2hdc, (G) 2hdc, (A) 2hdc, (H) 2hdc, (A) 2hdc, (B) 22hdc.

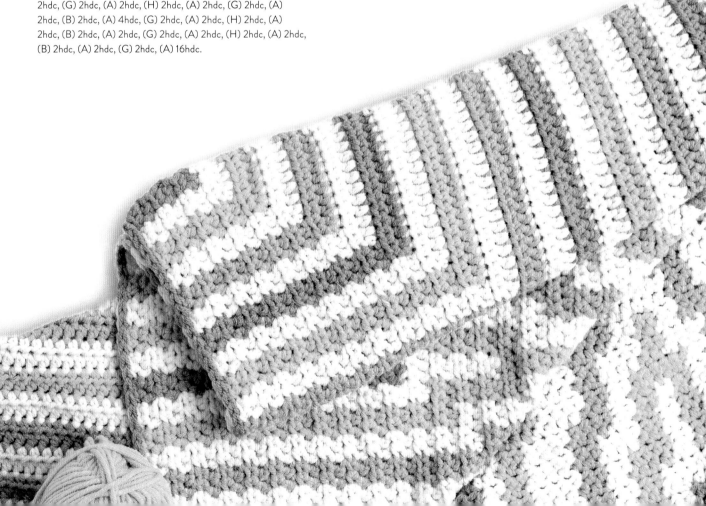

Rows 27 and 28: (A) Ch1, 24hdc, (H) 2hdc, (A) 2hdc, (G) 2hdc, (A) 2hdc, (B) 2hdc, (A) 2hdc, (H) 2hdc, (A) 2hdc, (G) 2hdc, (A) 4hdc, (B) 2hdc, (A) 4hdc, (G) 2hdc, (A) 2hdc, (G) 2hdc, (A) 4hdc, (B) 2hdc, (A) 4hdc, (G) 2hdc, (A) 2hdc, (H) 2hdc, (A) 2hdc, (B) 2hdc, (A) 2hdc, (G) 2hdc, (A) 2hdc, (H) 2hdc, (A) 24hdc.

Rows 29 and 30: (H) Ch1, 26hdc, (A) 2hdc, (G) 2hdc, (A) 2hdc, (B) 2hdc, (A) 2hdc, (H) 2hdc, (A) 2hdc, (G) 2hdc, (A) 4hdc, (B) 4hdc, (A) 2hdc, (G) 2hdc, (A) 2hdc, (G) 2hdc, (A) 2hdc, (B) 4hdc, (A) 4hdc, (G) 2hdc, (A) 2hdc, (H) 2hdc, (A) 2hdc, (B) 2hdc, (A) 2hdc, (G) 2hdc, (A) 2hdc, (H) 26hdc.

Rows 31 and 32: (A) Ch1, 28hdc, (G) 2hdc, (A) 2hdc, (B) 2hdc, (A) 2hdc, (H) 2hdc, (A) 2hdc, (G) 4hdc, (A) 4hdc, (B) 2hdc, (A) 2hdc, (G) 6hdc, (A) 2hdc, (B) 2hdc, (A) 4hdc, (G) 4hdc, (A) 2hdc, (H) 2hdc, (A) 2hdc, (B) 2hdc, (A) 2hdc, (G) 2hdc, (A) 28hdc.

Rows 33 and 34: (G) Ch1, 30hdc, (A) 2hdc, (B) 2hdc, (A) 2hdc, (H) 2hdc, (A) 4hdc, (G) 2hdc, (A) 4hdc, (B) 2hdc, (A) 4hdc, (G) 2hdc, (A) 4hdc, (B) 2hdc, (A) 4hdc, (G) 2hdc, (A) 4hdc, (H) 2hdc, (A) 2hdc, (B) 2hdc, (A) 2hdc, (G) 30hdc.

Rows 35 and 36: (A) Ch1, 32hdc, (B) 2hdc, (A) 2hdc, (H) 4hdc, (A) 2hdc, (G) 2hdc, (A) 4hdc, (B) 4hdc, (A) 2hdc, (G) 2hdc, (A) 2hdc, (B) 4hdc, (A) 4hdc, (G) 2hdc, (A) 2hdc, (H) 4hdc, (A) 2hdc, (B) 2hdc, (A) 32hdc.

Rows 37 and 38: (B) Ch1, 34hdc, (A) 4hdc, (H) 2hdc, (A) 2hdc, (G) 4hdc, (A) 4hdc, (B) 2hdc, (A) 6hdc, (B) 2hdc, (A) 4hdc, (G) 4hdc, (A) 2hdc, (H) 2hdc, (A) 4hdc, (B) 34hdc.

Rows 39 and 40: (A) Ch1, 38hdc, (H) 2hdc, (A) 4hdc, (G) 2hdc, (A) 4hdc, (B) 4hdc, (A) 2hdc, (B) 4hdc, (A) 4hdc, (G) 2hdc, (A) 4hdc, (H) 2hdc, (A) 38hdc.

Rows 41 and 42: (H) Ch1, 34hdc, (A) 4hdc, (H) 4hdc, (A) 2hdc, (G) 4hdc, (A) 4hdc, (B) 2hdc, (A) 2hdc, (B) 2hdc, (A) 4hdc, (G) 4hdc, (A) 2hdc, (H) 4hdc, (A) 4hdc, (H) 34hdc.

Rows 43 and 44: (A) Ch1, 32hdc, (H) 10hdc, (A) 4hdc, (G) 2hdc, (A) 4hdc, (B) 6hdc, (A) 4hdc, (G) 2hdc, (A) 4hdc, (H) 10hdc, (A) 32hdc.

Rows 45 and 46: (G) Ch1, 30hdc, (A) 8hdc, (H) 6hdc, (A) 2hdc, (G) 4hdc, (A) 4hdc, (B) 2hdc, (A) 4hdc, (G) 4hdc, (A) 2hdc, (H) 6hdc, (A) 8hdc, (G) 30hdc.

Rows 47 and 48: (A) Ch1, 28hdc, (G) 8hdc, (A) 6hdc, (H) 2hdc, (A) 4hdc, (G) 2hdc, (A) 10hdc, (G) 2hdc, (A) 4hdc, (H) 2hdc, (A) 6hdc, (G) 8hdc, (A) 28hdc.

Rows 49 and 50: (A) Ch1, 34hdc, (G) 6hdc, (A) 8hdc, (G) 4hdc, (A) 6hdc, (G) 4hdc, (A) 8hdc, (G) 6hdc, (A) 34hdc.

Rows 51 and 52: (B) Ch1, 28hdc, (A) 10hdc, (G) 6hdc, (A) 6hdc, (G) 4hdc, (A) 2hdc, (G) 4hdc, (A) 6hdc, (G) 6hdc, (A) 10hdc, (B) 28hdc.

Rows 53 and 54: (A) Ch1, 26hdc, (B) 8hdc, (A) 8hdc, (G) 6hdc, (A) 4hdc, (G) 2hdc, (A) 2hdc, (G) 2hdc, (A) 4hdc, (G) 6hdc, (A) 8hdc, (B) 8hdc, (A) 26hdc.

Rows 55 and 56: (H) Ch1, 24hdc, (A) 8hdc, (B) 6hdc, (A) 8hdc, (G) 6hdc, (A) 2hdc, (H) 2hdc, (A) 2hdc, (G) 6hdc, (A) 8hdc, (B) 6hdc, (A) 8hdc, (H) 24hdc.

TIP

Read all the information in the book on how to manage your yarns (see Working Intarsia Crochet: Managing Yarns) and colour changes (see Intarsia Crochet: Changing Colours) before you start crocheting a blanket. The information is there to help and guide you and make the process easier.

Rows 57 and 58: Repeat Rows 53 and 54.

Rows 59 and 60: Repeat Rows 51 and 52.

Rows 61 and 62: Repeat Rows 49 and 50.

Rows 63 and 64: Repeat Rows 47 and 48.

Rows 65 and 66: Repeat Rows 45 and 46.

Rows 67 and 68: Repeat Rows 43 and 44.

Rows 69 and 70: Repeat Rows 41 and 42.

Rows 71 and 72: Repeat Rows 39 and 40.

Rows 73 and 74: Repeat Rows 37 and 38.

Rows 75 and 76: Repeat Rows 35 and 36.

Rows 77 and 78: Repeat Rows 33 and 34.

Rows 79 and 80: Repeat Rows 31 and 32.

Rows 81 and 82: Repeat Rows 29 and 30.

Rows 83 and 84: Repeat Rows 27 and 28.

Rows 85 and 86: Repeat Rows 25 and 26.

Rows 87 and 88: Repeat Rows 23 and 24.

Rows 89 and 90: Repeat Rows 21 and 22.

Rows 91 and 92: Repeat Rows 19 and 20.

Rows 93 and 94: Repeat Rows 17 and 18.

Rows 95 and 96: Repeat Rows 15 and 16.

Rows 97 and 98: Repeat Rows 13 and 14.

Rows 99 and 100: Repeat Rows 11 and 12.

Rows 101 and 102: Repeat Rows 9 and 10.

Rows 103 and 104: Repeat Rows 7 and 8.

Rows 105 to 110: Repeat Rows 1 to 6.

Don't break yarn.

Row 111 (RS): (H) 110 sl sts across to the end.

Fasten off, and sew in all yarn ends.

Add tassels or pompoms if desired.

WORKING FROM CHART

For each row, work all stitches from
1 to 110. Work Rows 1 to 110 once,
Continue with Row 111 of written
instructions.

KEY

☐ Buttercream Icing

▦ Cotton Candy Meringue

▦ Mint Whoopie Pie

▦ Bubblegum Ice Cream

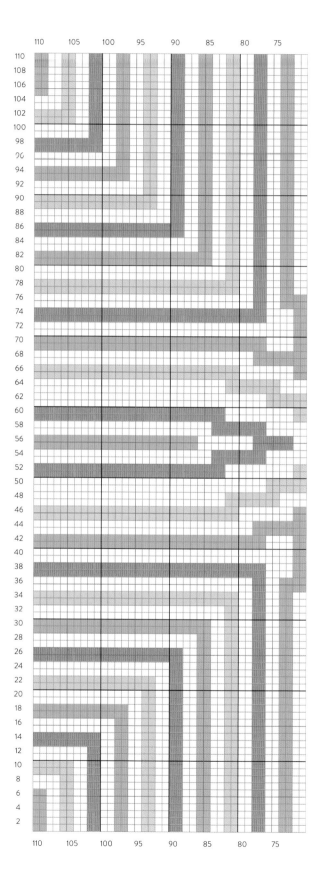

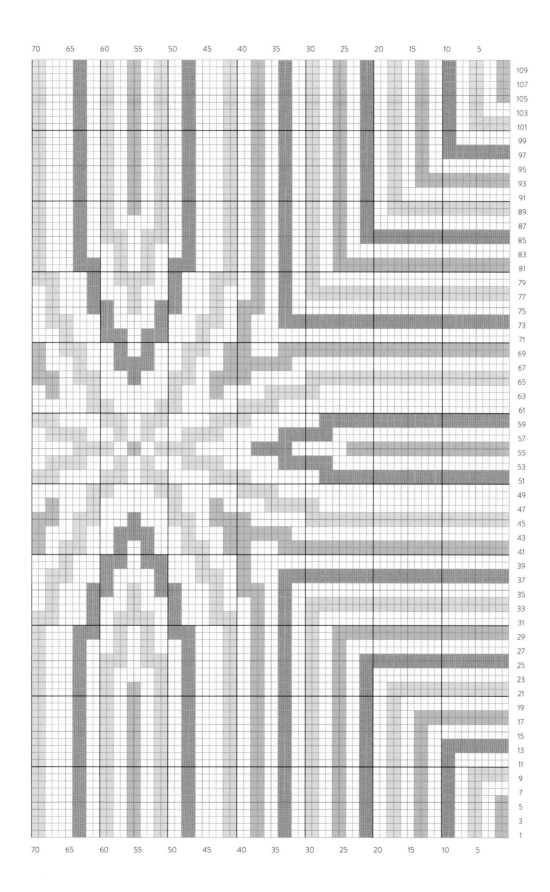

SHIFTING
SQUARES

The mesmerizing overlapping squares in this design create an effective three-dimensional impression. It almost looks as if it has been assembled from three strips, instead of crocheted in one piece.

YOU WILL NEED

HOOK

6.5mm (US K/10.5) hook

YARN

Scheepjes Truly Scrumptious (50% recycled polyester (recycled plastic bottles) and 50% acrylic), aran (worsted) weight, 100g (3½oz) = 108m (118yd), in the following shades:

- A: Buttercream Icing (302) x 6 balls
- B: Cotton Candy Meringue (330) x 2 balls
- D: Orange Cheesecake (332) x 2 balls
- G: Mint Whoopie Pie (340) x 3 balls
- J: Lavender Slice (334) x 2 balls

YARN BALLS WOUND

- A: 26 x 23g (¾oz)
- B: 6 x 33g (1⅙oz)
- D: 6 x 33g (1⅙oz)
- G: 6 x 50g (1¾oz)
- J: 6 x 33g (1⅙oz)

TENSION (GAUGE)

11 stitches x 9 rows = 10cm (4in) square

FINISHED SIZE

125 x 96cm (49 x 38in)

PATTERN

Using a 6.5mm (US K/10.5) hook, chain 111 in Yarn A. Now start in the 2nd chain from the hook.

Rows 1 and 2: (A) Ch1, 2hdc, (G) 2hdc, (A) 2hdc, (B) 2hdc, (A) 2hdc, (D) 20hdc, (A) 2hdc, (B) 2hdc, (A) 2hdc, (G) 2hdc, (D) 10hdc, (A) 2hdc, (J) 2hdc, (A) 2hdc, (G) 2hdc, (A) 2hdc, (J) 2hdc, (A) 2hdc, (D) 10hdc, (G) 2hdc, (A) 2hdc, (B) 2hdc, (A) 2hdc, (D) 20hdc, (A) 2hdc, (B) 2hdc, (A) 2hdc, (G) 2hdc, (A) 2hdc. (110 sts)

Rows 3 and 4: (A) Ch1, 2hdc, (G) 2hdc, (A) 2hdc, (B) 2hdc, (A) 24hdc, (B) 2hdc, (A) 2hdc, (G) 2hdc, (A) 12hdc, (J) 2hdc, (A) 2hdc, (G) 2hdc, (A) 2hdc, (J) 2hdc, (A) 12hdc, (G) 2hdc, (A) 2hdc, (B) 2hdc, (A) 24hdc, (B) 2hdc, (A) 2hdc, (G) 2hdc, (A) 2hdc.

Rows 5 and 6: (A) Ch1, 2hdc, (G) 2hdc, (A) 2hdc, (B) 28hdc, (A) 2hdc, (G) 2hdc, (J) 14hdc, (A) 2hdc, (G) 2hdc, (A) 2hdc, (J) 14hdc, (G) 2hdc, (A) 2hdc, (B) 28hdc, (A) 2hdc, (G) 2hdc, (A) 2hdc.

Rows 7 and 8: (A) Ch1, 2hdc, (G) 2hdc, (A) 32hdc, (G) 2hdc, (A) 16hdc, (G) 2hdc, (A) 16hdc, (G) 2hdc, (A) 32hdc, (G) 2hdc, (A) 2hdc.

Rows 9 and 10: (G) Ch1, 110hdc.

Rows 11 and 12: (A) Ch1, 1hdc, (G) 2hdc, (A) 16hdc, (G) 2hdc, (A) 16hdc, (G) 2hdc, (A) 32hdc, (G) 2hdc, (A) 16hdc, (G) 2hdc, (A) 16hdc, (G) 2hdc, (A) 1hdc.

Rows 13 and 14: (A) Ch1, 1hdc, (G) 2hdc, (J) 14hdc, (A) 2hdc, (G) 2hdc, (A) 2hdc, (J) 14hdc, (G) 2hdc, (A) 2hdc, (B) 28hdc, (A) 2hdc, (G) 2hdc, (J) 14hdc, (A) 2hdc, (G) 2hdc, (A) 2hdc, (J) 14hdc, (G) 2hdc, (A) 1hdc.

Rows 15 and 16: (A) Ch1, 1hdc, (G) 2hdc, (A) 12hdc, (J) 2hdc, (A) 2hdc, (G) 2hdc, (A) 2hdc, (J) 2hdc, (A) 12hdc, (G) 2hdc, (A) 2hdc, (B) 2hdc, (A) 24hdc, (B) 2hdc, (A) 2hdc, (G) 2hdc, (A) 12hdc, (J) 2hdc, (A) 2hdc, (G) 2hdc, (A) 2hdc, (J) 2hdc, (A) 12hdc, (G) 2hdc, (A) 1hdc.

Rows 17 and 18: (A) Ch1, 1hdc, (G) 2hdc, (D) 10hdc, (A) 2hdc, (J) 2hdc, (A) 2hdc, (G) 2hdc, (A) 2hdc, (J) 2hdc, (A) 2hdc, (D) 10hdc, (G) 2hdc, (A) 2hdc, (B) 2hdc, (A) 2hdc, (D) 20hdc, (A) 2hdc, (B) 2hdc, (A) 2hdc, (G) 2hdc, (D) 10hdc, (A) 2hdc, (J) 2hdc, (A) 2hdc, (G) 2hdc, (A) 2hdc, (J) 2hdc, (A) 2hdc, (D) 10hdc, (G) 2hdc, (A) 1hdc.

Rows 19 and 20: (A) Ch1, 1hdc, (G) 2hdc, (A) 8hdc, (D) 2hdc, (A) 2hdc, (J) 2hdc, (A) 2hdc, (G) 2hdc, (A) 2hdc, (J) 2hdc, (A) 2hdc, (D) 2hdc, (A) 8hdc, (G) 2hdc, (A) 2hdc, (B) 2hdc, (A) 2hdc, (D) 2hdc, (A) 16hdc, (D) 2hdc, (A) 2hdc, (B) 2hdc, (A) 2hdc, (G) 2hdc, (A) 8hdc, (D) 2hdc, (A) 2hdc, (J) 2hdc, (A) 2hdc, (G) 2hdc, (A) 2hdc, (J) 2hdc, (A) 2hdc, (D) 2hdc, (A) 8hdc, (G) 2hdc, (A) 1hdc.

Rows 21 and 22: (A) Ch1, 1hdc, (G) 2hdc, (B) 6hdc, (A) 2hdc, (D) 2hdc, (A) 2hdc, (J) 2hdc, (A) 2hdc, (G) 2hdc, (A) 2hdc, (J) 2hdc, (A) 2hdc, (D) 2hdc, (A) 2hdc, (B) 6hdc, (G) 2hdc, (A) 2hdc, (B) 2hdc, (A) 2hdc, (D) 2hdc, (A) 2hdc, (J) 12hdc, (A) 2hdc, (D) 2hdc, (A) 2hdc, (B) 2hdc, (A) 2hdc, (G) 2hdc, (B) 6hdc, (A) 2hdc, (D) 2hdc, (A) 2hdc, (J) 2hdc, (A) 2hdc, (G) 2hdc, (A) 2hdc, (J) 2hdc, (A) 2hdc, (D) 2hdc, (A) 2hdc, (B) 6hdc, (G) 2hdc, (A) 1hdc.

Rows 23 and 24: (A) Ch1, 1hdc, (G) 2hdc, (A) 4hdc, (B) 2hdc, (A) 2hdc, (D) 2hdc, (A) 2hdc, (J) 2hdc, (A) 2hdc, (G) 2hdc, (A) 2hdc, (J) 2hdc, (A) 2hdc, (D) 2hdc, (A) 2hdc, (B) 2hdc, (A) 4hdc, (G) 2hdc, (A) 2hdc, (B) 2hdc, (A) 2hdc, (D) 2hdc, (A) 2hdc, (J) 2hdc, (A) 8hdc, (J) 2hdc, (A) 2hdc, (D) 2hdc, (A) 2hdc, (B) 2hdc, (A) 2hdc, (G) 2hdc, (A) 4hdc, (B) 2hdc, (A) 2hdc, (D) 2hdc, (A) 2hdc, (J) 2hdc, (A) 2hdc, (G) 2hdc, (A) 2hdc, (J) 2hdc, (A) 2hdc, (D) 2hdc, (A) 2hdc, (B) 2hdc, (A) 4hdc, (G) 2hdc, (A) 1hdc.

Rows 25 to 28: (A) Ch1, 1hdc, (G) 4hdc, (A) 2hdc, (B) 2hdc, (A) 2hdc, (D) 2hdc, (A) 2hdc, (J) 2hdc, (A) 2hdc, (G) 2hdc, (A) 2hdc, (J) 2hdc, (A) 2hdc, (D) 2hdc, (A) 2hdc, (B) 2hdc, (A) 2hdc, (G) 4hdc, (A) 2hdc, (B) 2hdc, (A) 2hdc, (D) 2hdc, (A) 2hdc, (J) 2hdc, (A) 2hdc, (G) 4hdc, (A) 2hdc, (J) 2hdc, (A) 2hdc, (D) 2hdc, (A) 2hdc, (B) 2hdc, (A) 2hdc, (G) 4hdc, (A) 2hdc, (B) 2hdc, (A) 2hdc, (D) 2hdc, (A) 2hdc, (J) 2hdc, (A) 2hdc, (G) 2hdc, (A) 2hdc, (J) 2hdc, (A) 2hdc, (D) 2hdc, (A) 2hdc, (B) 2hdc, (A) 2hdc, (G) 4hdc, (A) 1hdc.

Rows 29 and 30: Repeat Rows 23 and 24.

Rows 31 and 32: Repeat Rows 21 and 22.

Rows 33 and 34: Repeat Rows 19 and 20.

Rows 35 and 36: Repeat Rows 17 and 18.

Rows 37 and 38: Repeat Rows 15 and 16.

Rows 39 and 40: Repeat Rows 13 and 14.

Rows 41 and 42: Repeat Rows 11 and 12.

Rows 43 and 44: Repeat Rows 9 and 10.

Rows 45 and 46: Repeat Rows 7 and 8.

Rows 47 and 48: Repeat Rows 5 and 6.

Rows 49 and 50: Repeat Rows 3 and 4.

Rows 51 and 52: Repeat Rows 1 and 2.

Rows 53 and 54: (A) Ch1, 2hdc, (G) 2hdc, (A) 2hdc, (B) 2hdc, (A) 2hdc, (D) 2hdc, (A) 16hdc, (D) 2hdc, (A) 2hdc, (B) 2hdc, (A) 2hdc, (G) 2hdc, (A) 8hdc, (D) 2hdc, (A) 2hdc, (J) 2hdc, (A) 2hdc, (G) 2hdc, (A) 2hdc, (J) 2hdc, (A) 2hdc, (D) 2hdc, (A) 8hdc, (G) 2hdc, (A) 2hdc, (B) 2hdc, (A) 2hdc, (D) 2hdc, (A) 16hdc, (D) 2hdc, (A) 2hdc, (B) 2hdc, (A) 2hdc, (G) 2hdc, (A) 2hdc.

Rows 55 and 56: (A) Ch1, 2hdc, (G) 2hdc, (A) 2hdc, (B) 2hdc, (A) 2hdc, (D) 2hdc, (A) 2hdc, (J) 12hdc, (A) 2hdc, (D) 2hdc, (A) 2hdc, (B) 2hdc, (A) 2hdc, (G) 2hdc, (B) 6hdc, (A) 2hdc, (D) 2hdc, (A) 2hdc, (J) 2hdc, (A) 2hdc, (G) 2hdc, (A) 2hdc, (J) 2hdc, (A) 2hdc, (D) 2hdc, (A) 2hdc, (B) 6hdc, (G) 2hdc, (A) 2hdc, (B) 2hdc, (A) 2hdc, (D) 2hdc, (A) 2hdc, (J) 12hdc, (A) 2hdc, (D) 2hdc, (A) 2hdc, (B) 2hdc, (A) 2hdc, (G) 2hdc, (A) 2hdc.

Rows 57 and 58: (A) Ch1, 2hdc, (G) 2hdc, (A) 2hdc, (B) 2hdc, (A) 2hdc, (D) 2hdc, (A) 2hdc, (J) 2hdc, (A) 8hdc, (J) 2hdc, (A) 2hdc, (D) 2hdc, (A) 2hdc, (B) 2hdc, (A) 2hdc, (G) 2hdc, (A) 4hdc, (B) 2hdc, (A) 2hdc, (D) 2hdc, (A) 2hdc, (J) 2hdc, (A) 2hdc, (G) 2hdc, (A) 2hdc, (J) 2hdc, (A) 2hdc, (D) 2hdc, (A) 2hdc, (B) 2hdc, (A) 4hdc, (G) 2hdc, (A) 2hdc, (B) 2hdc, (A) 2hdc, (D) 2hdc, (A) 2hdc, (J) 2hdc, (A) 8hdc, (J) 2hdc, (A) 2hdc, (D) 2hdc, (A) 2hdc, (B) 2hdc, (A) 2hdc, (G) 2hdc, (A) 2hdc.

Rows 59 to 62: (A) Ch1, 2hdc, (G) 2hdc, (A) 2hdc, (B) 2hdc, (A) 2hdc, (D) 2hdc, (A) 2hdc, (J) 2hdc, (A) 2hdc, (G) 4hdc, (A) 2hdc, (J) 2hdc, (A) 2hdc, (D) 2hdc, (A) 2hdc, (B) 2hdc, (A) 2hdc, (G) 4hdc, (A) 2hdc, (B) 2hdc, (A) 2hdc, (D) 2hdc, (A) 2hdc, (J) 2hdc, (A) 2hdc, (G) 2hdc, (A) 2hdc, (J) 2hdc, (A) 2hdc, (D) 2hdc, (A) 2hdc, (B) 2hdc, (A) 2hdc, (G) 4hdc, (A) 2hdc, (B) 2hdc, (A) 2hdc, (D) 2hdc, (A) 2hdc, (J) 2hdc, (A) 2hdc, (G) 4hdc, (A) 2hdc, (J) 2hdc, (A) 2hdc, (D) 2hdc, (A) 2hdc, (B) 2hdc, (A) 2hdc, (G) 2hdc, (A) 2hdc.

Rows 63 and 64: (A) Ch1, 2hdc, (G) 2hdc, (A) 2hdc, (B) 2hdc, (A) 2hdc, (D) 2hdc, (A) 2hdc, (J) 2hdc, (A) 8hdc, (J) 2hdc, (A) 2hdc, (D) 2hdc, (A) 2hdc, (B) 2hdc, (A) 2hdc, (G) 2hdc, (A) 4hdc, (B) 2hdc, (A) 2hdc, (D) 2hdc, (A) 2hdc, (J) 2hdc, (A) 2hdc, (G) 2hdc, (A) 2hdc, (J) 2hdc, (A) 2hdc, (D) 2hdc, (A) 2hdc, (B) 2hdc, (A) 4hdc, (G) 2hdc, (A) 2hdc, (B) 2hdc, (A) 2hdc, (D) 2hdc, (A) 2hdc, (J) 2hdc, (A) 8hdc, (J) 2hdc, (A) 2hdc, (D) 2hdc, (A) 2hdc, (B) 2hdc, (A) 2hdc, (G) 2hdc, (A) 2hdc.

Rows 65 and 66: (A) Ch1, 2hdc, (G) 2hdc, (A) 2hdc, (B) 2hdc, (A) 2hdc, (D) 2hdc, (A) 2hdc, (J) 12hdc, (A) 2hdc, (D) 2hdc, (A) 2hdc, (B) 2hdc, (A) 2hdc, (G) 2hdc, (B) 6hdc, (A) 2hdc, (D) 2hdc, (A) 2hdc, (J) 2hdc, (A) 2hdc, (G) 2hdc, (A) 2hdc, (J) 2hdc, (A) 2hdc, (D) 2hdc, (A) 2hdc, (B) 6hdc, (G) 2hdc, (A) 2hdc, (B) 2hdc, (A) 2hdc, (D) 2hdc, (A) 2hdc, (J) 12hdc, (A) 2hdc, (D) 2hdc, (A) 2hdc, (B) 2hdc, (A) 2hdc, (G) 2hdc, (A) 2hdc.

Rows 67 and 68: (A) Ch1, 2hdc, (G) 2hdc, (A) 2hdc, (B) 2hdc, (A) 2hdc, (D) 2hdc, (A) 16hdc, (D) 2hdc, (A) 2hdc, (B) 2hdc, (A) 2hdc, (G) 2hdc, (A) 8hdc, (D) 2hdc, (A) 2hdc, (J) 2hdc, (A) 2hdc, (G) 2hdc, (A) 2hdc, (J) 2hdc, (A) 2hdc, (D) 2hdc, (A) 8hdc, (G) 2hdc, (A) 2hdc, (B) 2hdc, (A) 2hdc, (D) 2hdc, (A) 16hdc, (D) 2hdc, (A) 2hdc, (B) 2hdc, (A) 2hdc, (G) 2hdc, (A) 2hdc.

Rows 69 to 120: Repeat Rows 1 to 52.

Don't break yarn.

Row 121 (RS): (A) 110 sl sts across to the end.

Fasten off, and sew in all yarn ends.

Add tassels or pompoms if desired.

WORKING FROM CHART

For each row, work all stitches from 1 to 110. Work Rows 1 to 68 once, then repeat Rows 1 to 52 once more. Continue with Row 121 of written instructions.

KEY

 Buttercream Icing

Cotton Candy Meringue

Orange Cheesecake

Mint Whoopie Pie

Lavender Slice

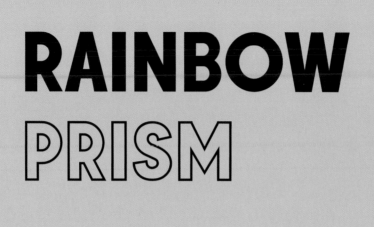

RAINBOW
PRISM

The curved edges of the central elongate diamond in this design seem to project forwards in front of the striped backdrop. The effect is almost like bands of light deflected through a prism.

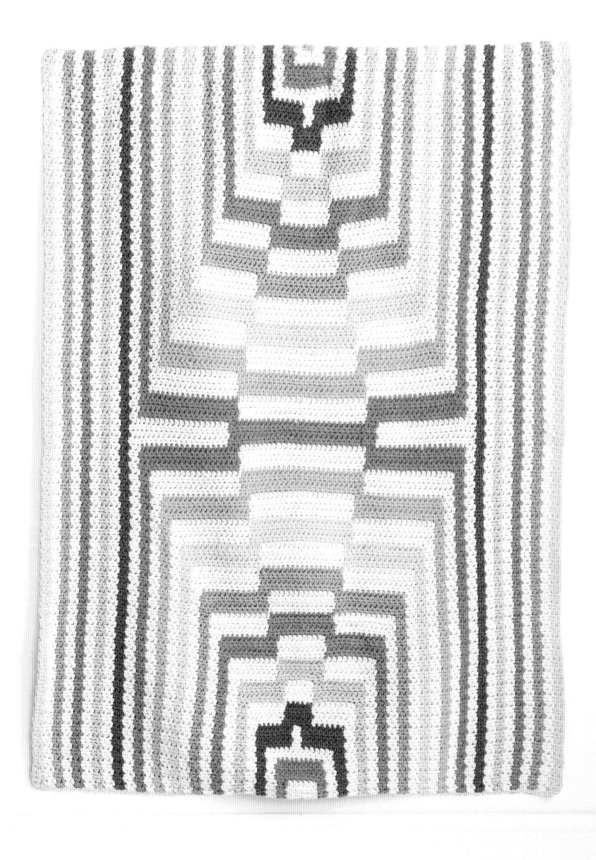

YOU WILL NEED

HOOK

6.5mm (US K/10.5) hook

YARN

Scheepjes Truly Scrumptious (50% recycled polyester (recycled plastic bottles) and 50% acrylic), aran (worsted) weight, 100g (3½oz) = 108m (118yd), in the following shades:

- A: Buttercream Icing (302) x 7 balls
- C: Rose Barfi (321) x 2 balls
- D: Orange Cheesecake (332) x 1 ball
- E: Custard Pie (341) x 2 balls
- F: Pistachio Bundt Cake (318) x 2 balls
- H: Bubblegum Ice Cream (355) x 2 balls
- I: French Blue Macaron (343) x 1 ball
- K: Sweet Potato Mochi (320) x 1 ball

YARN BALLS WOUND

- A: 26 x 26g (⅞oz)
- C: 4 x 50g (1¾oz)
- D: 3 x 33g (1⅛oz)
- E: 4 x 50g (1¾oz)
- F: 4 x 50g (1¾oz)
- H: 4 x 50g (1¾oz)
- I: 4 x 25g (⅞oz)
- K: 4 x 25g (⅞oz)

TENSION (GAUGE)

11 stitches x 9 rows = 10cm (4in) square

FINISHED SIZE

130 x 93cm (51 x 36½in)

PATTERN

Using a 6.5mm (US K/10.5) hook, chain 107 in Yarn E. Now start in the 2nd chain from the hook.

Rows 1 and 2: (E) Ch1, 2hdc, (A) 2hdc, (F) 2hdc, (A) 2hdc, (H) 2hdc, (A) 2hdc, (I) 2hdc, (A) 2hdc, (K) 2hdc, (A) 2hdc, (C) 2hdc, (A) 2hdc, (D) 2hdc, (A) 2hdc, (E) 2hdc, (A) 2hdc, (F) 2hdc, (A) 2hdc, (H) 2hdc, (A) 2hdc, (I) 2hdc, (A) 2hdc, (K) 2hdc, (A) 2hdc, (C) 2hdc, (A) 2hdc, (D) 2hdc, (A) 2hdc, (C) 2hdc, (A) 2hdc, (K) 2hdc, (A) 2hdc, (I) 2hdc, (A) 2hdc, (H) 2hdc, (A) 2hdc, (F) 2hdc, (A) 2hdc, (E) 2hdc, (A) 2hdc, (D) 2hdc, (A) 2hdc, (C) 2hdc, (A) 2hdc, (K) 2hdc, (A) 2hdc, (I) 2hdc, (A) 2hdc, (H) 2hdc, (A) 2hdc, (F) 2hdc, (A) 2hdc, (E) 2hdc. (106 sts)

Rows 3 and 4: (E) Ch1, 2hdc, (A) 2hdc, (F) 2hdc, (A) 2hdc, (H) 2hdc, (A) 2hdc, (I) 2hdc, (A) 2hdc, (K) 2hdc, (A) 2hdc, (C) 2hdc, (A) 2hdc, (D) 2hdc, (A) 2hdc, (E) 2hdc, (A) 2hdc, (F) 2hdc, (A) 2hdc, (H) 2hdc, (A) 2hdc, (I) 2hdc, (A) 2hdc, (K) 2hdc, (A) 2hdc, (C) 2hdc, (A) 6hdc, (C) 2hdc, (A) 2hdc, (K) 2hdc, (A) 2hdc, (I) 2hdc, (A) 2hdc, (H) 2hdc, (A) 2hdc, (F) 2hdc, (A) 2hdc, (E) 2hdc, (A) 2hdc, (D) 2hdc, (A) 2hdc, (C) 2hdc, (A) 2hdc, (K) 2hdc, (A) 2hdc, (I) 2hdc, (A) 2hdc, (H) 2hdc, (A) 2hdc, (F) 2hdc, (A) 2hdc, (E) 2hdc.

Rows 5 to 8: (E) Ch1, 2hdc, (A) 2hdc, (F) 2hdc, (A) 2hdc, (H) 2hdc, (A) 2hdc, (I) 2hdc, (A) 2hdc, (K) 2hdc, (A) 2hdc, (C) 2hdc, (A) 2hdc, (D) 2hdc, (A) 2hdc, (E) 2hdc, (A) 2hdc, (F) 2hdc, (A) 2hdc, (H) 2hdc, (A) 2hdc, (I) 2hdc, (A) 2hdc, (K) 2hdc, (A) 2hdc, (C) 10hdc, (A) 2hdc, (K) 2hdc, (A) 2hdc, (I) 2hdc, (A) 2hdc, (H) 2hdc, (A) 2hdc, (F) 2hdc, (A) 2hdc, (E) 2hdc, (A) 2hdc, (D) 2hdc, (A) 2hdc, (C) 2hdc, (A) 2hdc, (K) 2hdc, (A) 2hdc, (I) 2hdc, (A) 2hdc, (H) 2hdc, (A) 2hdc, (F) 2hdc, (A) 2hdc, (E) 2hdc.

Rows 9 and 10: (E) Ch1, 2hdc, (A) 2hdc, (F) 2hdc, (A) 2hdc, (H) 2hdc, (A) 2hdc, (I) 2hdc, (A) 2hdc, (K) 2hdc, (A) 2hdc, (C) 2hdc, (A) 2hdc, (D) 2hdc, (A) 2hdc, (E) 2hdc, (A) 2hdc, (F) 2hdc, (A) 2hdc, (H) 2hdc, (A) 2hdc, (I) 2hdc, (A) 2hdc, (K) 2hdc, (A) 14hdc, (K) 2hdc, (A) 2hdc, (I) 2hdc, (A) 2hdc, (H) 2hdc, (A) 2hdc, (F) 2hdc, (A) 2hdc, (E) 2hdc, (A) 2hdc, (D) 2hdc, (A) 2hdc, (C) 2hdc, (A) 2hdc, (K) 2hdc, (A) 2hdc, (I) 2hdc, (A) 2hdc, (H) 2hdc, (A) 2hdc, (F) 2hdc, (A) 2hdc, (E) 2hdc.

Rows 11 to 14: (E) Ch1, 2hdc, (A) 2hdc, (F) 2hdc, (A) 2hdc, (H) 2hdc, (A) 2hdc, (I) 2hdc, (A) 2hdc, (K) 2hdc, (A) 2hdc, (C) 2hdc, (A) 2hdc, (D) 2hdc, (A) 2hdc, (E) 2hdc, (A) 2hdc, (F) 2hdc, (A) 2hdc, (H) 2hdc, (A) 2hdc, (I) 2hdc, (A) 2hdc, (K) 8hdc, (A) 2hdc, (K) 8hdc, (A) 2hdc, (I) 2hdc, (A) 2hdc, (H) 2hdc, (A) 2hdc, (F) 2hdc, (A) 2hdc, (E) 2hdc, (A) 2hdc, (D) 2hdc, (A) 2hdc, (C) 2hdc, (A) 2hdc, (K) 2hdc, (A) 2hdc, (I) 2hdc, (A) 2hdc, (H) 2hdc, (A) 2hdc, (F) 2hdc, (A) 2hdc, (E) 2hdc.

Rows 15 to 18: (E) Ch1, 2hdc, (A) 2hdc, (F) 2hdc, (A) 2hdc, (H) 2hdc, (A) 2hdc, (I) 2hdc, (A) 2hdc, (K) 2hdc, (A) 2hdc, (C) 2hdc, (A) 2hdc, (D) 2hdc, (A) 2hdc, (E) 2hdc, (A) 2hdc, (F) 2hdc, (A) 2hdc, (H) 2hdc, (A) 2hdc, (I) 2hdc, (A) 8hdc, (K) 6hdc, (A) 8hdc, (I) 2hdc, (A) 2hdc, (H) 2hdc, (A) 2hdc, (F) 2hdc, (A) 2hdc, (E) 2hdc, (A) 2hdc, (D) 2hdc, (A) 2hdc, (C) 2hdc, (A) 2hdc, (K) 2hdc, (A) 2hdc, (I) 2hdc, (A) 2hdc, (H) 2hdc, (A) 2hdc, (F) 2hdc, (A) 2hdc, (E) 2hdc.

Rows 19 to 22: (E) Ch1, 2hdc, (A) 2hdc, (F) 2hdc, (A) 2hdc, (H) 2hdc, (A) 2hdc, (I) 2hdc, (A) 2hdc, (K) 2hdc, (A) 2hdc, (C) 2hdc, (A) 2hdc, (D) 2hdc, (A) 2hdc, (E) 2hdc, (A) 2hdc, (F) 2hdc, (A) 2hdc, (H) 2hdc, (A) 2hdc, (I) 10hdc, (A) 6hdc, (I) 10hdc, (A) 2hdc, (H) 2hdc, (A) 2hdc, (F) 2hdc, (A) 2hdc, (E) 2hdc, (A) 2hdc, (D) 2hdc, (A) 2hdc, (C) 2hdc, (A) 2hdc, (K) 2hdc, (A) 2hdc, (I) 2hdc, (A) 2hdc, (H) 2hdc, (A) 2hdc, (F) 2hdc, (A) 2hdc, (E) 2hdc.

Rows 23 to 26: (E) Ch1, 2hdc, (A) 2hdc, (F) 2hdc, (A) 2hdc, (H) 2hdc, (A) 2hdc, (I) 2hdc, (A) 2hdc, (K) 2hdc, (A) 2hdc, (C) 2hdc, (A) 2hdc, (D) 2hdc, (A) 2hdc, (E) 2hdc, (A) 2hdc, (F) 2hdc, (A) 2hdc, (H) 2hdc, (A) 10hdc, (I) 10hdc, (A) 10hdc, (H) 2hdc, (A) 2hdc, (F) 2hdc, (A) 2hdc, (E) 2hdc, (A) 2hdc, (D) 2hdc, (A) 2hdc, (C) 2hdc, (A) 2hdc, (K) 2hdc, (A) 2hdc, (I) 2hdc, (A) 2hdc, (H) 2hdc, (A) 2hdc, (F) 2hdc, (A) 2hdc, (E) 2hdc.

Rows 27 to 30: (E) Ch1, 2hdc, (A) 2hdc, (F) 2hdc, (A) 2hdc, (H) 2hdc, (A) 2hdc, (I) 2hdc, (A) 2hdc, (K) 2hdc, (A) 2hdc, (C) 2hdc, (A) 2hdc, (D) 2hdc, (A) 2hdc, (E) 2hdc, (A) 2hdc, (F) 2hdc, (A) 2hdc, (H) 12hdc, (A) 10hdc, (H) 12hdc, (A) 2hdc, (F) 2hdc, (A) 2hdc, (E) 2hdc, (A) 2hdc, (D) 2hdc, (A) 2hdc, (C) 2hdc, (A) 2hdc, (K) 2hdc, (A) 2hdc, (I) 2hdc, (A) 2hdc, (H) 2hdc, (A) 2hdc, (F) 2hdc, (A) 2hdc, (E) 2hdc.

Rows 31 to 34: (E) Ch1, 2hdc, (A) 2hdc, (F) 2hdc, (A) 2hdc, (H) 2hdc, (A) 2hdc, (I) 2hdc, (A) 2hdc, (K) 2hdc, (A) 2hdc, (C) 2hdc, (A) 2hdc, (D) 2hdc, (A) 2hdc, (E) 2hdc, (A) 2hdc, (F) 2hdc, (A) 12hdc, (H) 14hdc, (A) 12hdc, (F) 2hdc, (A) 2hdc, (E) 2hdc, (A) 2hdc, (D) 2hdc, (A) 2hdc, (C) 2hdc, (A) 2hdc, (K) 2hdc, (A) 2hdc, (I) 2hdc, (A) 2hdc, (H) 2hdc, (A) 2hdc, (F) 2hdc, (A) 2hdc, (E) 2hdc.

Rows 35 to 38: (E) Ch1, 2hdc, (A) 2hdc, (F) 2hdc, (A) 2hdc, (H) 2hdc, (A) 2hdc, (I) 2hdc, (A) 2hdc, (K) 2hdc, (A) 2hdc, (C) 2hdc, (A) 2hdc, (D) 2hdc, (A) 2hdc, (E) 2hdc, (A) 2hdc, (F) 14hdc, (A) 14hdc, (F) 14hdc, (A) 2hdc, (E) 2hdc, (A) 2hdc, (D) 2hdc, (A) 2hdc, (C) 2hdc, (A) 2hdc, (K) 2hdc, (A) 2hdc, (I) 2hdc, (A) 2hdc, (H) 2hdc, (A) 2hdc, (F) 2hdc, (A) 2hdc, (E) 2hdc.

Rows 39 to 42: (E) Ch1, 2hdc, (A) 2hdc, (F) 2hdc, (A) 2hdc, (H) 2hdc, (A) 2hdc, (I) 2hdc, (A) 2hdc, (K) 2hdc, (A) 2hdc, (C) 2hdc, (A) 2hdc, (D) 2hdc, (A) 2hdc, (E) 2hdc, (A) 14hdc, (F) 18hdc, (A) 14hdc, (E) 2hdc, (A) 2hdc, (D) 2hdc, (A) 2hdc, (C) 2hdc, (A) 2hdc, (K) 2hdc, (A) 2hdc, (I) 2hdc, (A) 2hdc, (H) 2hdc, (A) 2hdc, (F) 2hdc, (A) 2hdc, (E) 2hdc.

Rows 43 to 46: (E) Ch1, 2hdc, (A) 2hdc, (F) 2hdc, (A) 2hdc, (H) 2hdc, (A) 2hdc, (I) 2hdc, (A) 2hdc, (K) 2hdc, (A) 2hdc, (C) 2hdc, (A) 2hdc, (D) 2hdc, (A) 2hdc, (E) 16hdc, (A) 18hdc, (E) 16hdc, (A) 2hdc, (D) 2hdc, (A) 2hdc, (C) 2hdc, (A) 2hdc, (K) 2hdc, (A) 2hdc, (I) 2hdc, (A) 2hdc, (H) 2hdc, (A) 2hdc, (F) 2hdc, (A) 2hdc, (E) 2hdc.

Rows 47 to 50: (E) Ch1, 2hdc, (A) 2hdc, (F) 2hdc, (A) 2hdc, (H) 2hdc, (A) 2hdc, (I) 2hdc, (A) 2hdc, (K) 2hdc, (A) 2hdc, (C) 2hdc, (A) 2hdc, (D) 2hdc, (A) 16hdc, (E) 22hdc, (A) 16hdc, (D) 2hdc, (A) 2hdc, (C) 2hdc, (A) 2hdc, (K) 2hdc, (A) 2hdc, (I) 2hdc, (A) 2hdc, (H) 2hdc, (A) 2hdc, (F) 2hdc, (A) 2hdc, (E) 2hdc.

Rows 51 to 54: (E) Ch1, 2hdc, (A) 2hdc, (F) 2hdc, (A) 2hdc, (H) 2hdc, (A) 2hdc, (I) 2hdc, (A) 2hdc, (K) 2hdc, (A) 2hdc, (C) 2hdc, (A) 2hdc, (D) 18hdc, (A) 22hdc, (D) 18hdc, (A) 2hdc, (C) 2hdc, (A) 2hdc, (K) 2hdc, (A) 2hdc, (I) 2hdc, (A) 2hdc, (H) 2hdc, (A) 2hdc, (F) 2hdc, (A) 2hdc, (E) 2hdc.

Rows 55 to 58: (E) Ch1, 2hdc, (A) 2hdc, (F) 2hdc, (A) 2hdc, (H) 2hdc, (A) 2hdc, (I) 2hdc, (A) 2hdc, (K) 2hdc, (A) 2hdc, (C) 2hdc, (A) 18hdc, (D) 26hdc, (A) 18hdc, (C) 2hdc, (A) 2hdc, (K) 2hdc, (A) 2hdc, (I) 2hdc, (A) 2hdc, (H) 2hdc, (A) 2hdc, (F) 2hdc, (A) 2hdc, (E) 2hdc.

Rows 59 to 62: (E) Ch1, 2hdc, (A) 2hdc, (F) 2hdc, (A) 2hdc, (H) 2hdc, (A) 2hdc, (I) 2hdc, (A) 2hdc, (K) 2hdc, (A) 2hdc, (C) 20hdc, (A) 26hdc, (C) 20hdc, (A) 2hdc, (K) 2hdc, (A) 2hdc, (I) 2hdc, (A) 2hdc, (H) 2hdc, (A) 2hdc, (F) 2hdc, (A) 2hdc, (E) 2hdc.

Rows 63 to 66: (E) Ch1, 2hdc, (A) 2hdc, (F) 2hdc, (A) 2hdc, (H) 2hdc, (A) 2hdc, (I) 2hdc, (A) 2hdc, (K) 2hdc, (A) 20hdc, (C) 30hdc, (A) 20hdc, (K) 2hdc, (A) 2hdc, (I) 2hdc, (A) 2hdc, (H) 2hdc, (A) 2hdc, (F) 2hdc, (A) 2hdc, (E) 2hdc.

TIPS

Using separate balls of yarn for each colour change helps you to transition from one colour to the next more easily.

I keep the balls of yarn attached to my blanket in a long basket so they are all in one place.

Rows 67 to 70: Repeat Rows 59 to 62.

Rows 71 to 74: Repeat Rows 55 to 58.

Rows 75 to 78: Repeat Rows 51 to 54.

Rows 79 to 82: Repeat Rows 47 to 50.

Rows 83 to 86: Repeat Rows 43 to 46.

Rows 87 to 90: Repeat Rows 39 to 42.

Rows 91 to 94: Repeat Rows 35 to 38.

Rows 95 to 98: Repeat Rows 31 to 34.

Rows 99 to 102: Repeat Rows 27 to 30.

Rows 103 to 106: Repeat Rows 23 to 26.

Rows 107 to 110: Repeat Rows 19 to 22.

Rows 111 to 114: Repeat Rows 15 to 18.

Rows 115 to 118: Repeat Rows 11 to 14.

Rows 119 and 120: Repeat Rows 9 and 10.

Rows 121 to 124: Repeat Rows 5 to 8.

Rows 125 and 126: Repeat Rows 3 and 4.

Rows 127 and 128: Repeat Rows 1 and 2.

Don't break yarn.

Row 129 (RS): (E) 106 sl sts across to the end.

Fasten off, and sew in all yarn ends.

Add tassels or pompoms if desired.

WORKING FROM CHART

For each row, work all stitches from 1 to 106. Work Rows 1 to 128 once. Continue with Row 129 of written instructions.

KEY

☐ Buttercream Icing

▥ Rose Barfi

▥ Orange Cheesecake

▥ Custard Pie

▥ Pistachio Bundt Cake

▥ Bubblegum Ice Cream

☐ French Blue Macaron

▥ Sweet Potato Mochi

TOP

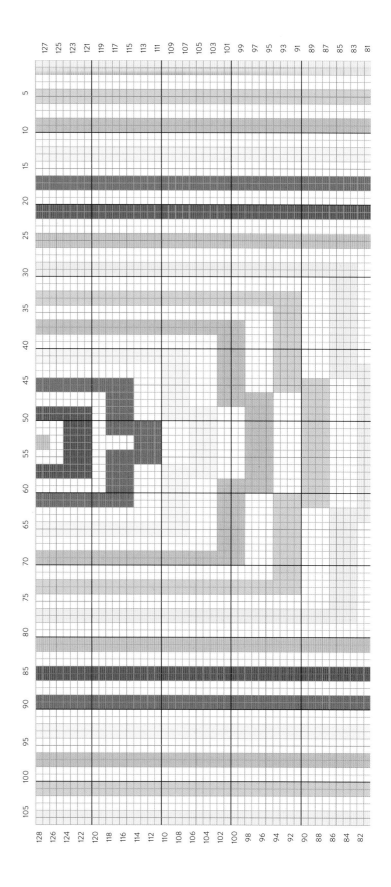

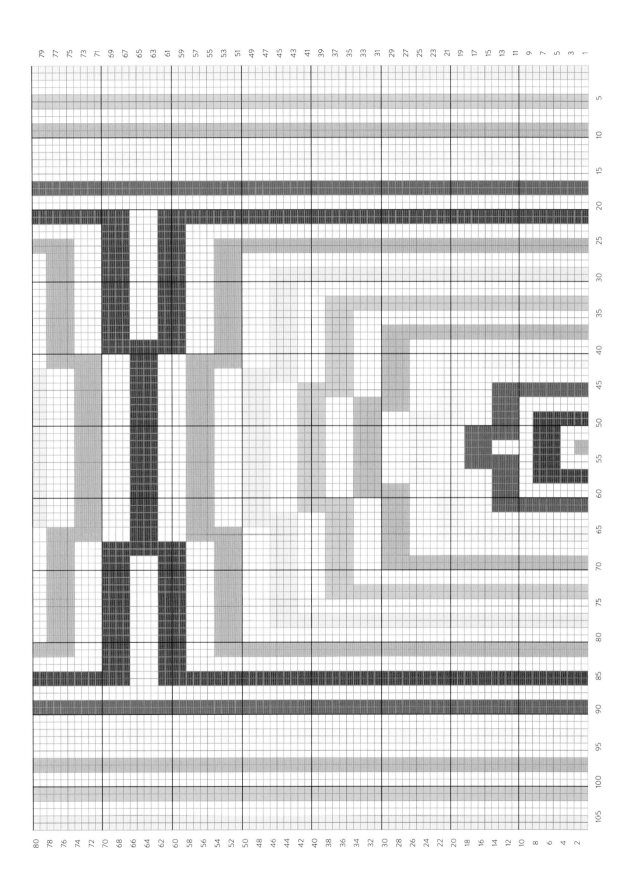

GENERAL TECHNIQUES

The techniques needed for the patterns in this book are basic stitches, so they are great projects for beginners as well for as more experienced crocheters. Some prior experience of colourwork or intarsia crochet would be a bonus but is not necessary, as everything is explained.

BASIC STITCHES

SLIP KNOT

This knot attaches the yarn to the hook. Make a loop in the yarn near the end, leaving a tail of about 15cm (6in). With your fingers or the hook, grab the ball-end of the yarn and draw it through the loop to the front (A). Pull both ends of the yarn to secure the knot around the hook. Do not pull too tightly, leave the slip knot slightly loose on the hook.

CHAIN (CH)

Begin with a slip knot on the hook. Hold the hook in your dominant hand and the base of the slip knot with the left thumb and forefinger of the other hand. Take the working yarn over the hook (B) and twist the hook anticlockwise to catch the yarn and pull it through the slip knot (C) to create a new chain stitch (D). Continue until you have the required number of chain stitches, gently pulling down on the chain as you go.

SLIP STITCH (SL ST)

Insert the hook into the stitch from front to back, yarn over (E). Pull the yarn through the stitch and through the loop on the hook (F).

HALF DOUBLE CROCHET (HDC)

Yarn over and insert the hook into the second chain from the hook (G), yarn over again and pull through the three loops on the hook (H) to complete the first stitch. Continue like this, working in each chain to the end of the first row (I). To begin the second row, chain one, yarn over, insert the hook into the top of the first stitch from front to back (J), yarn over and pull the yarn through the stitch (three loops on the hook) (K). Yarn over and pull through all three loops on the hook to finish the stitch (L).

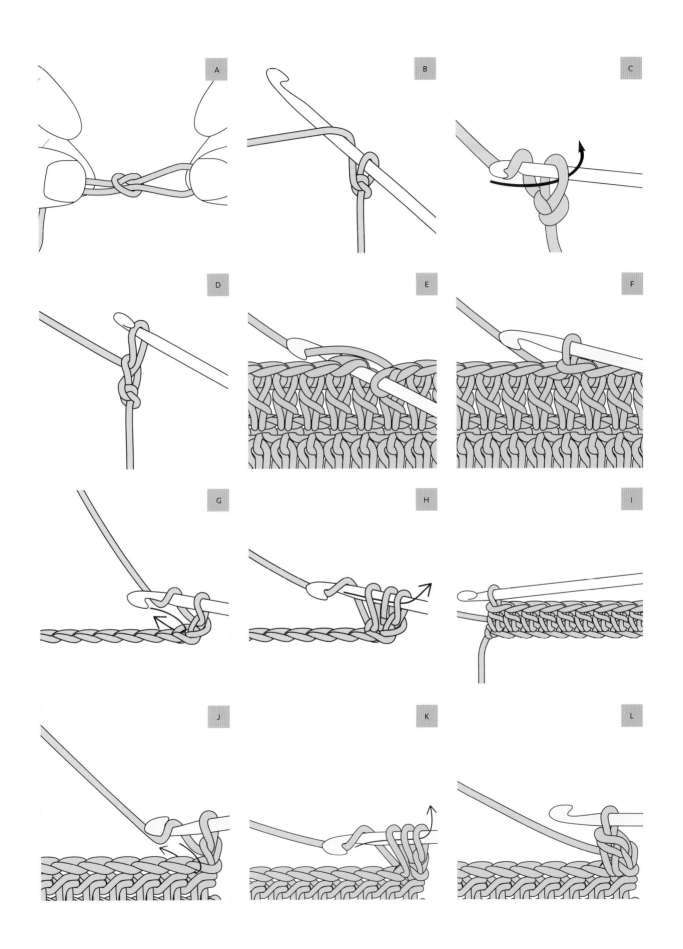

FINISHING OFF

Finishing off your blanket and making it look its best is my favourite part of making! Because of the illusion in the design of these blankets, I don't tend to add a border, but you can if you want to and I have included instructions (right). However, if there was no border I felt that something else needed to be added to make them look and feel finished. I decided pompoms and tassels were the best option – they are also super fun to make and the colour possibilities are endless, from using one solid colour to incorporating all the colours you have used for your blanket.

ADDING A BORDER

If you want to add a border to your blanket then here is a super simple one that uses the same stitch you have used throughout the book.

Join your chosen yarn to the top right hand corner of your blanket.

Round 1: Ch1, *hdc in each st across top of blanket, (2hdc, ch2, 2hdc) in last st (corner), work evenly down side alternating 1hdc and 2hdc in side of hdc rows, (2hdc, ch2, 2hdc) in last st (corner); repeat from * across bottom and second side, sl st in first hdc to join.

Round 2: Ch1, *1hdc in each st across top, (2hdc, ch2, 2hdc) in corner ch-2 space, 1hdc in each st down side, (2hdc, ch2, 1hdc) in corner ch-2 space; repeat from * across bottom and second side, sl st in first hdc to join.

Round 3: Repeat Round 2.

Fasten off and sew in ends.

TASSELS

You can use Yarn A for your tassels, or any yarn colour of your choice. Make four tassels and then trim them and attach to each corner of the blanket.

Cut a rectangle of sturdy cardstock, with the long side the desired length of the tassel (30cm/12in). Wrap the yarn around the card lengthways as many times as you like, depending on how full you want your tassel. Cut a length of yarn and slide it under all the loops at the top (A), then knot the ends securely to fasten – leave the ends long to join the tassel to the project. Cut through all the loops along the bottom edge (B) and remove the card. Wind another long length of yarn three times around all the strands (except the joining yarn at the top) just down from the top (C) and knot to secure. Trim the ends to the same length as the tassel strands.

POMPOMS

Using Yarn A, or the colour of your choice and a 7cm (2¾in) pompom maker, make four pompoms. Then trim them and attach them to each corner of the blanket.

If you don't have a pompom maker, a pompom can be made with two circles of cardstock. Cut two cardstock circles the desired diameter of the pompom and cut a circular opening in the middle to about a third of the diameter. Place the two circles together and wrap yarn around the outside (D) until the middle hole is filled. Slide the blade of a pair of scissors between the layers of card and cut the yarn all around the outside (E). Cut a long length of yarn and slide it between the card circles (F). Tie the two ends and knot very tightly to secure the pompom. Slide off the card circles, fluff up the pompom and trim to neaten if necessary. Use the long yarn ends to attach it to the project.

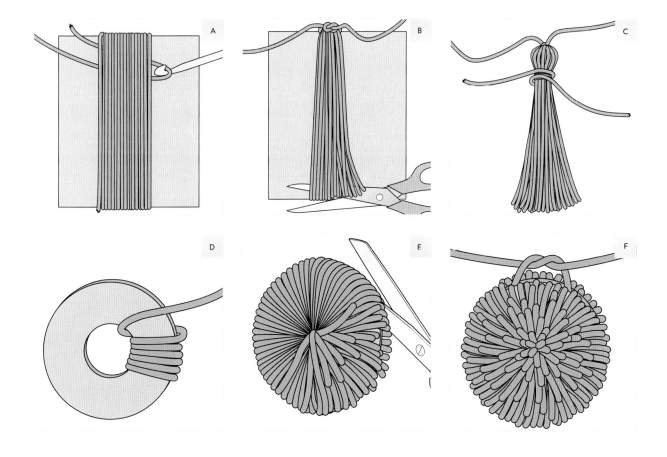

ABOUT THE AUTHOR

Helen Smith first became interested in crochet in 2016, and after she started designing blankets in 2020 during lockdown. She has designed for several magazines, yarn brands and subscription boxes, but this is her first book. She lives in Skipton, North Yorkshire with her husband, two children and two little dogs. Helen was born at RAF Lyneham where her family were based because her dad was in the RAF at the time. Both grandparents from her mum's side were Polish and Helen and her older sister Amanda were brought up with lots of Polish cuisine, which Helen loves to cook. Unfortunately Amanda was diagnosed with MS when she was only 21, which declined rapidly after a fall in 2020, so Helen and her mum soon became carers. Crochet has definitely been Helen's escape over the last few years, helping her get through tough times. Find her on:

Instagram: www.instagram.com/emkatcrochet
Facebook: www.facebook.com/emkatcrochetx

THANKS

A HUGE thank you to my wonderful husband, Graham. Thank you for letting me keep literally hundreds of balls of yarn all over the house and for not complaining even when you were tripping up over them – thanks also for fetching them down from the loft when needed! I will be forever grateful for the support and understanding I have received from you and our two beautiful girls, Katie and Emily. You have encouraged me to continue on this journey and have been with me every step of the way. The blankets in this book have been part of our lives for months and are now part of our family, even coming on holiday with us! Thank you also to my mum, for always being there through everything, for looking after Amanda the way you do and yet still finding time to help and encourage me to carry on. Finally, thank you to all my friends and family for your love, support, inspiration and encouragement.

DEDICATION

I am dedicating this book to my sister. She has been my inspiration throughout the process of writing it and is truly one in a million for going through what she goes through every day and to still be smiling. 'You are my number one, Amanda, and will always be forever in my heart, *Kocham cię* (I love you)!'

SUPPLIERS

Thank you to Scheepjes for kindly supplying all the yarn needed to create these beautiful blankets.

INDEX

A DAVID AND CHARLES BOOK
© David and Charles, Ltd 2024

David and Charles is an imprint of David and Charles, Ltd
Suite A, Tourism House, Pynes Hill, Exeter, EX2 5WS

ISBN-13: 9781446312698 paperback
ISBN-13: 9781446312711 EPUB
ISBN-13: 9781446312704 PDF

This book has been printed on paper from approved suppliers and made from pulp from sustainable sources.

FSC
www.fsc.org
MIX
Paper from responsible sources
FSC® C012521

Printed in China through Asia Pacific Offset for:
David and Charles, Ltd
Suite A, Tourism House, Pynes Hill, Exeter, EX2 5WS

10 9 8 7 6 5 4 3 2 1

Publishing Director: Ame Verso
Senior Commissioning Editor: Sarah Callard
Managing Editor: Jeni Chown
Project Editors: Marie Clayton and Lindsay Kaubi
Technical Editor: Sam Winkler
Head of Design: Anna Wade
Designers: Sam Staddon and Jo Webb
Pre press Designer: Susan Reansbury
Illustrations: Kuo Kang Chen
Art Direction: Laura Woussen
Photography: Jason Jenkins
Production Manager: Beverley Richardson

David and Charles publishes high-quality books on a wide range of subjects. For more information visit www.davidandcharles.com.

Share your makes with us on social media using #dandcbooks and follow us on Facebook and Instagram by searching for @dandcbooks.

Layout of the digital edition of this book may vary depending on reader hardware and display settings.